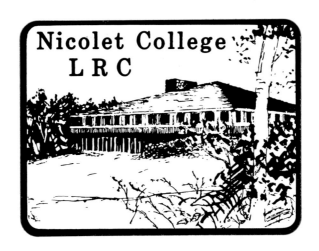

Nicolet College
L R C

DATE DUE

WRITE IT ON YOUR HEART
The Epic World of an Okanagan Storyteller

WRITE IT ON YOUR HEART

The Epic World of an Okanagan Storyteller

Harry Robinson

Compiled and Edited by Wendy Wickwire

Talonbooks/Theytus   •   Vancouver   •   1989

published with the assistance of the Canada Council

Financially assisted by the Ministry of Municipal Affairs, Recreation and Culture through the British Columbia Heritage Trust and B.C. Lotteries

Talonbooks
210/1019 East Cordova
Vancouver,
British Columbia, V6A 1M8
Canada

Typeset in Cheltenham and Sabon by Piéce de Résistance Ltée and printed and bound in Canada by Hignell Printing Ltd.

Some of these stories appeared in slightly different form in *Canadian Fiction Magazine,* and *Whetstone.*

All photographs (including covers) are by Robert Semeniuk. The front cover photograph is of a pictograph near Ashnola River in the Similkameen Valley. The photograph of Harry and Margaret Holding (1922), Harry and his dog (1927), and Harry and Matilda (1948) are courtesy of Harry Robinson.

First printing September 1989.

Canadian Cataloguing in Publication Data
Robinson, Harry, 1900-
   Write it on your heart

  ISBN 0-88922-273-8

  1. Indians of North America - Legends. I. Wickwire,
Wendy C. II. Title.
E98.F6R62 1989   398.2'08997   C88-091596-X

To the Okanagan people

CONTENTS

INTRODUCTION

It was a blazing hot August afternoon when I first met Harry Robinson. It was the summer of 1977 and two friends had invited me to accompany them on a trip with Harry to the annual Omak rodeo in Washington State. He was very happy to see us when we arrived at his small house beside the highway near Hedley. As I was to discover was his custom, he invited us all to sit with him around the arborite table which stood prominently in the centre of his clean and ordered living room. While we were chatting during dinner, some element in the conversation suddenly prompted Harry to launch into a story. The story continued for several hours until well past midnight.

The next day we all set off for Omak and the rodeo. But this, my first experience of a true traditional storyteller has drawn me back to Harry again and again, year after year. In addition to his wealth of stories, many exciting and moving adventures were to follow—rodeos, sacred winter dances, and walks to his favourite mythological sites. Here in this quiet setting beside the Similkameen River in British Columbia's southern interior, in a neat and simple house without television, radio or newspapers, Harry lives with an unbroken contact to a deep past. It has been a privilege—and a most enjoyable one—to spend time with him.

THE MAKING OF A STORYTELLER

Harry was born on October 8th, 1900 at Oyama, in the Okanagan Valley near Kelowna. Along with many other seasonal workers, his mother, Arcell Newhmkin, and her parents had stopped there temporarily to earn some money digging and packing potatoes. When the work was done, they moved on with their new baby to their home near Chopaka, in the Similkameen Valley near Keremeos.

Members of the Lower Similkameen Indian Band, Harry's mother and her family were of full Okanagan ancestry. The Okanagan Indian reserves cover a huge territory, from the upper end of Okanagan Lake in the north, to Brewster, Washington in the south. Their language belongs to the Interior division of the Salishan language family. In south central British Columbia, this division also includes the Shuswap, Lillooet, and Thompson languages.

The Similkameen Valley has not always been occupied by Okanagan-speaking people. Research conducted in the late 1800s shows that an Athapaskan-speaking people, possibly related to the Chilcotin people in the north, once occupied this country as well as the Nicola Valley to the north.

Exactly what these "Similkameen-Nicola Athapaskans," as they have come to be known, were like and where they came from remains a mystery. As early as about 1700 they began to be absorbed by the Thompson and Okanagan-speaking peoples. By 1900 their language was nearly extinct and, by 1940 almost all memory of this culture was gone. In the Similkameen Valley today, only Okanagan is spoken and the most elderly natives acknowledge only that at one time the "Similkameen" language, not the "Okanagan" language, was spoken by the people who lived in this valley.[1]

---

1. Randy Bouchard and Dorothy Kennedy, "Indian History and Knowledge of the Lower Similkameen River-Palmer Lake area." Report prepared for the United States Army Corps of Engineers, Seattle District, October, 1984.

11

Harry's father, Jimmie Robinson, was born in Ashnola in the Similkameen Valley, of an Okanagan mother and a Scottish father. Arcell and Jimmie had parted ways before their son was born, so Harry spent his childhood years with Arcell and her parents, Louise and Joseph Newhmkin, at their small ranch near Chopaka.

Louise was almost seventy years old and partially blind when her grandson was born. She had been raised in Brewster, south of the border, but had moved to Chopaka after her marriage in 1852. While Arcell worked to support the small family, Harry looked after his grandmother, and during their many hours together, she began to tell him stories which would later become the centre and meaning of his life:

> Somebody's got to be with her all the time. And when we're together just by ourselves, she'd tell me, "Come here!" And I sit here while she hold me. And she'd tell me stories, kinda slow. She wanted me to understand good. For all that time until I got to be big, she tell me stories. She tell me stories until she die in 1918 when she was eighty-five.

Harry's storytelling circle was larger than just his grandmother. He speaks of others, including, for example, old Mary Narcisse, who was reputed to be 116 when she died in 1944, and John Ashnola, with whom Harry lived for almost a year when he was fourteen. "Every night when I come in from working, he always tell me stories until late." John Ashnola died in the 1918 flu epidemic at the age of ninety-eight. Other names figure prominently as well. Alex Skeuce, old Pierre, and old Christine, who was blind, are just some of the oldtimers who passed their stories on to Harry: "I got enough people to tell me. That's why I know."

There was a small public school in Cawston, another village in the same area, and for five months, at the age of thirteen, Harry made the daily twelve-mile return trip to attend. But the trip was exhausting, and he soon stopped his public-school education. Only later, when he was twenty-two, did he learn to read and write with the assistance of a friend, Margaret Holding.

Ranching was the major way of life in the Similkameen Valley of Harry's youth and, to him, learning the skills of raising cattle was more important than acquiring a formal education. For his first job as a ranch-hand in January of 1917, he fed 580 head of cattle and 10 horses for two months. The following year, in March, he worked as a packer for a local sheep camp. That winter he fed the sheep (all 1800 of them) in addition to 80 head of cattle and 30 horses, staying on with the camp until 1919. That year, however, hearing that an older rancher, Bert Allison, needed workers, Harry went to him in search of a job and Allison placed him in charge of his hayfield. It was a tough job. As Harry describes it, "I piled sixteen to eighteen stacks of hay—that's about 400 tons." He stayed with Allison until 1920, and for the next few years he took on a variety of jobs, such as cutting wood near Summerland, clearing land, feeding stock, and baling hay.

Finally, through marriage, Harry acquired his first ranch. The year was 1924, and he was working for a local rancher, Felix Johnny, breaking horses. Hearing that one of his mother's neighbours had died suddenly while bronco-riding, Harry took one of the horses and rode to the funeral.

While at the funeral at Chopaka, Harry realized that the man's widow, Matilda, would make a good wife for him. Although she was about ten years older than he, she was a good cook, a good gardener, and an experienced rancher.

Her family was well known to Harry. Matilda, like her mother before her, had been born and raised in Chopaka. Her father, John Shiweelkin, had been raised at Ashnola, but had later moved to Chopaka where he ran a prosperous ranch of up to 300 head of cattle. Matilda had had the same traditional upbringing as Harry's mother and grandmother.

Harry, at twenty-four, was tired of wandering from job to job with no base of his own. Settling down with Matilda looked very attractive to him and, not long after the funeral, he approached her about marriage. At first she declined his offers saying that he was too young and footloose. But finally Harry's persistence and promises to be a good and loyal husband won her over. They took the train from Chopaka to Oroville, where she ordered him to go to the second-hand store to buy a suit (his first), and there, on December 9, 1924, they were married by a priest.

Harry now had a secure home of his own in the place where he had spent his childhood. With Matilda, he expanded their ranch by working for other ranchers in the area, feeding cattle, planting potatoes, and doing odd jobs. Through buying, selling, and trading cows and horses, Harry and Matilda had, by the mid-1950s, acquired four large ranches between Chopaka and Ashnola, with 60 horses and 150 head of cattle. As he says, "I feed stock from January 2, 1917 until 1972—over fifty years I feed cattle without missing a day in feeding season, rain or shine, snow or blizzards, Sundays, holidays and funerals."

In 1956, a hip injury began to slow Harry down. He and Matilda had not had any children to assist them, so they had to hire help. Over the years they had gradually sold their cattle. By the time of Matilda's death on March 26, 1971, they had scaled down their ranch to fifty head of cattle. After her death, Harry found it very difficult to run the ranch and his affairs alone. Two years later, he sold everything and rented a small bungalow near Hedley on the property of his longtime friends, Slim and Carrie Allison.

Leading such a strenuous life, Harry had been so busy that he had had little time or inclination for telling stories. "I don't care for it," he explains, "and I forget." As his life slowed down, however, those hours and hours of stories he had heard as a child began to come back. Matilda had encouraged this, for, as Harry puts it, "she's got a good head, and she's the one that tell me, her dad, the things he knows."

Advancing age actually seemed to stimulate his storytelling ability. By his late seventies he remarked that, "The older I get, it seems to come back on me. It's like pictures going by. I could see and remember." Even today, bed-ridden, frail, and in pain, his capacity to remember is enormous. On my most recent visit with him in Keremeos in early May of this year, he seemed very pleased to be able to launch once more into a story. As always, it included the smallest details.

Harry has always had a precise mind and a startling memory. He has often berated me when I have forgotten a detail which he had told me years earlier. One time he told me that he could tell stories for "twenty-one hours or more" when he got

13

started. "Kinda hard to believe," he continued, "but I do, because this is my job. I'm a storyteller."

THE MAKING OF A COLLECTION

For most of us in the 1980s, life is a hurried treadmill, but in Harry's home in the Similkameen, the silence is broken only by the ticking of The Regulator, his old-fashioned wall clock, and by conversation. Harry's life is filled not with material things, but with the pervasive presence of a still-living mythological world. Every hill, valley, canyon, creek, and river has its story.

In October of 1982, Harry travelled to Vancouver to undergo several weeks of medical treatment for a leg ulcer under the care of an elderly Chinese herbalist. Only then did the depth of Harry's mythological world become truly apparent to me. As we passed through downtown Vancouver on his visits to the doctor, I realized that all the traffic lights and automobiles meant nothing to Harry. They were almost an abstraction, an interesting but fleeting diversion from the timeless real world of Coyote, Fox and Owl.

With each visit, our relationship grew. Harry was alone, and although always occupied with some project (meticulously recorded on his memory lists), he enjoyed visitors, and I had the time to sit and listen.

On my many visits to him I usually took the bus from Vancouver to arrive on the highway near Harry's house. Whenever I did, I would be met by Harry sitting in the cab of his pick-up truck at the entrance to his driveway. His courtesy always extended to saving me the short walk to his house with my luggage. Even when I'd arrive in my old station wagon, Harry would be there waiting for me and my German Shepherd, Rufus. On such occasions there was always a special sleeping place prepared inside the house for Rufus.

It was my job to make dinner. Usually after an hour or so of catching up on the news, Harry would initiate a story. As his hearing was slightly impaired, two-way exchanges were somewhat strained. He was more relaxed in a one-way telling situation than he was in trying to decipher my end of the conversation.

His favourite time for stories is in the evening, so we spent the daylight hours doing errands and visiting favourite landmarks and friends. Harry loves the rodeos during the spring and summer, and the winter dances—the *shnay-WUM*[2], or "powwows" as he calls them in English, and whenever we could, we travelled to these. Between January and March of 1981 we attended all-night traditional Okanagan winter dance ceremonies from Penticton, British Columbia, to Omak, Washington.

Almost from the beginning, Harry and I both realized the importance of recording his stories. In his lifetime Harry has seen substantial change—horse and foot-trails have given way to paved highways, and rail lines have been constructed in one decade, only to be ripped out several decades later when the automobile replaced the train.

---

2. The linguistic transcriptions throughout are rough approximations only.

"Everything is changed . . . some of them changed to be all right, but some of them changed not good . . . . I think way back is better than now. Old days lots of fish. Go out before supper, half an hour before supper, go out on the river and come back with several trout. But nowadays you go over there, get nothing. You wouldn't get any. No fish there."

More than anything, Harry laments the erosion of his native language, and the replacement of storytelling by television and radio. In the Similkameen Valley, English is rapidly replacing the Okanagan language. In Harry's view, he is one of the last of the old storytellers. "I'm going to disappear," he says, "and there'll be no more telling stories."

As more and more of his listeners, native included, understood only English, Harry began telling his old stories in English to keep them alive. By the time I met him in 1977, he had become as skilled a storyteller in English as he had been in his native tongue.

With each passing year, my collection of recordings of Harry's stories increased until finally, on one visit, I approached him with the idea of turning some of them into a book. He responded with delight, as if this had been a long-time desire of his own. It was one way to leave his people with this testament to their past.

A book of stories told in English by a native Canadian storyteller is most unusual. Most published native stories are English translations done by someone other than the storyteller. Often these are not even direct translations, but rather extensively edited English summaries—sometimes an hour of oral telling is condensed to a page or two of print.

Such editing has often drawn criticism. The contemporary American poet Gary Snyder, who has done much to alert white audiences to the wisdom of native American ways, argues for maintaining the original, unedited story so that the readers can "do the editing with [their] imagination[s], rather than let someone else's imagination do the work for [them]." Snyder continues:

> I'm still dubious about what happens when modern white men start changing the old texts, making versions, editing, cleaning it up—not cleaning it up so much as just changing it around a little bit. There's nothing for me as useful as the direct transcription, as literally close as possible to the original text . . . . The true flavour seems to be there.[3]

As the editor of this collection, I have tried to present the stories exactly as told. In only two instances have I changed Harry's original. First, in speaking English, Harry uses pronouns indiscriminately. "He," "she," "it," and "they" are interchangeable, no matter what the antecedent. In most cases, Harry uses the plural neuter "they," rather than the singular "he," "she," or "it." This is common in the English speech of native elders, and when one is used to it, it does not cloud the story line. However, in order to minimize confusion for readers new to these stories, I have edited the pronouns to make them consistent with their antecedents.

---

3. Gary Snyder, *The Old Ways* (San Francisco: City Lights Books, 1977): 81-82.

Second, in a few cases where, due to an interruption, a short segment of a story is repeated verbatim, I have deleted it.

Beyond these editorial changes, I searched for a presentational style to capture the nuance of the oral tradition—the emphasis on certain phrases, intentional repetition, and dramatic rhythms and pauses. I have, therefore, set the stories in lines which mirror as closely as possible Harry's rhythms of speech. Harry's stories are really performed events, rather than fixed objects on a page, and are conveyed much better by shorter lines rather than by the standard short story prose style, in which line breaks are only a typographic convention.

Harry's repertory of stories is huge. In twelve years, I have recorded well over one hundred of them and this is but a fraction of what Harry knows. The stories in this book are representative of only the stories he has told me over the years, and of course, a number of factors have influenced his selection process. Harry no doubt told stories which he thought I, as a white, middle-class female, would like to (and should!) hear. Hence, there is not an instance of sexual innuendo or sexual exploits in the stories he told me. Stories which he tells to a young native male might be quite different. Harry also knew that I was very interested in native power, so he told me many power stories. In general, however, I did not try to influence his own selection and I believe the stories to be a good cross-section of his full repertory.

Most collectors of native North American stories have published what they have believed to be the purest of the most traditional stories. For instance, often those stories laden with post-contact references, or stories about the activities of post-contact white society have been excluded. In this collection, however, my objective has been to present a representative cross-section of Harry's repertory—including references to God, Heaven, and Hell, and "Puss in Boots."

All the stories are considered true stories. In fact, Harry, in the tradition of Okanagan storytelling, would never dream of making up a story. Stories describe either situations experienced personally or they describe situations passed on by others who similarly experienced them, however long ago. In the case of the latter, Harry simply explains, "this is the way I heard the stories so I tell it that way."

Harry makes a distinction between stories which are *chap-TEEK-whl* and those which are *shmee-MA-ee*. *Chap-TEEK-whl* are stories which explain how and why the world and its creatures came to be. They come from way back, from a pre-human mythological age when the Okanagan people were not yet fully human, but partook of both animal and human characteristics. Harry calls these first ancestors "animal-people." In contrast, *shmee-MA-ee* are stories from the age which followed the mythical age. They come from the more recent period, the world as we know it today, a world when "it's come to be real person, human people, instead of animal-people." Some of these stories occurred long ago, "before Christ," and before the white man, but after the time of the animal-people. This category also includes stories which occurred in more recent historical time.

16

BEGINNINGS: THE AGE OF THE ANIMAL-PEOPLE

The stories in Part One of the book are *chap-TEEK-whl*. All are part of a longer, loosely knit but continuous story-cycle. Some explain how the world and its people were created; others tell of the exploits of Coyote, the culture hero/trickster figure of the Okanagan people.

Creation Mythology: A Living Worldview

The creation myth which begins this book was originally told as one story. However, for the ease of the reader, I have divided it into three stories. With its intertwining of Christian and ancient native themes, this story offers interesting possibilities for interpretation. While this introduction is not the place for such analysis—this is a book of native stories, not a non-native analysis of the stories—a few points are worth considering briefly.

The God or "Big Chief" of Harry's story, like the Judeo-Christian God, is the creator and arranger of the world, the spiritual being through whom all life springs. Like the Old Testament God, Harry's Big Chief "thinks," and whatever he wishes appears. Just as the Judeo-Christian God gives Moses the covenant, the God of Harry's mythology gives the first people a paper instructing them how to live. Almost in the very words of the Old Testament, Harry's God tells his first people, prior to throwing them to faraway places, "You going to have increase."

But there are also obvious older, non-Judeo-Christian elements running through Harry's origin story. The most notable is the earth diver story. Its main motifs— earth covered by water, a creator, divers, the making of the earth from a grain of sand—represent a widely shared vision among native Americans from California, the Great Basin, the Plains, the Eastern Woodlands, to the Atlantic coast.[4]

There is little trace of the earth diver creation story in the published Okanagan creation stories. In fact, the anthropologist, Walter Cline, who worked among the Okanagans of Washington State in 1930, found that although they believed that the universe had been created by a supreme God, they had no story per se of creation.[5] Among the unpublished Okanagan story collections, however, there is at least one earth diver story. In June, 1969, the linguist, Randy Bouchard, recorded an earth diver story told by Selina Timoyakin of Penticton which is almost identical to that told by Harry.[6]

In addition, the published creation stories reveal a lot of variation in belief. One Okanagan story, recorded south of the border just after the turn of the century, explains that "Old One" or "Chief" made the earth out of a woman. The earth was and still is, therefore, alive. The soil is her flesh and the trees and vegetation her hair. Old One made the first people, who were animal-people, out of her flesh.[7]

---

4. Maria Leach, ed. *The Standard Dictionary of Folklore, Mythology, and Legend* (New York: Funk and Wagnalls Co., 1949) Vol.1: 334.

5. Walter Cline, "Religion and Worldview," in *The Sinkaietk or Southern Okanagon of Washington*, ed. Leslie Spier, (General Series in Anthropology, No. 6, Menasha, 1938): 176.

6. Randy Bouchard, Unpublished Fieldnotes, British Columbia Indian Language Project, Victoria, B.C., 1969.

7. James Teit, Marion K. Gould, Livingston Farrand and Herbert Spinden, "Folk-Tales of Salishan and Sahaptin Tribes," *Memoirs of the American Folk-Lore Society* 11: 80.

An Okanagan Lake storyteller explained to James Teit at the turn of the century that "the Chief (or God)" made seven worlds of which the earth is the central one. He too believed that the earth was a woman and the first people her flesh.[8] Another storyteller from the Similkameen Valley stated that "the Chief Above made the earth." It was small and he continued to roll it out until it was large. Then he created the animals, and at last he created a man who was also a wolf. From the man's tail he created a woman. These were the first people.[9]

This variation may be confusing to some. Yet, it must be understood, any knowledge of creation does not originate with the present teller, nor, indeed with a teller many hundreds of generations back. What we have, in these stories, is the result of an active, living, cultural process of storytelling; all we can know about creation is what these stories and people tell us about creation *now*. And there is a commonality here, for implicit in these Okanagan creation stories is a respectful, often reverential, assertion of the never-ending presence of "creation" in the present world. This contrasts markedly with the external, frozen concept of God and creation found in cultures which use *writing* to transmit these stories.

In the Christian tradition, God never manifests directly in physical form. God's "presence" may be felt, but the act of creation is in the past. In Harry's creation story, God stands on one of the leaves floating on the surface of the water, next to the five people he has just created. Harry explains: "Six man. They got five and himself. They got six." It would seem from Harry's description that God looks very much like his first people. The main difference between God and the others is that God is older and has more power.

In fact, God appears a number of times in Harry's stories. When Coyote goes to get a name, he finds the "Big Chief" sitting in a shedlike structure all by himself so as not to get wet. Later, God appears in disguise as a very old man with white hair when Coyote meets him and challenges him to a test of power. Finally, in "Prophecy at Lytton," God appears before the old woman and her grandson as a very old man. God is everywhere present, physically involved in the continuing product and act of creation.

Like the earth diver, another distinctly non-Christian element in Harry's story is the creation of the earth from something already existing. According to Harry's story of creation, the earth is present in the form of a tiny grain which lies below the surface of the already existing body of water. This image is common to the tradition of native American creation mythology where something is rarely created from nothing.[10] Creation always is.

The Early Influence of Christianity

Christian ideas had a profound impact upon the native worldview during the early years of white contact. The Spokane Indians, a related group to the southeast, were reported in 1825 to be holding ceremonies where they knelt on the ground before

8. Ibid: 84.
9. Ibid.
10. *The Standard Dictionary of Folklore* Vol. 2: 1134.

a religious picture which had been obtained from the traders. They also sang hymns and asked in their prayers to be saved from "the Black One Down Below."[11] In a trader's journal from Fort Coville in 1830, it was reported that the Indians at the Fort danced and prayed on Sundays in honour of "the Great Master of Life."[12] Also, in 1831, a Spokane Indian who became known as Spokane Garry, returned to his people from the Red River area where he had been indoctrinated in the Christian faith. He built a church and held services on Sundays and was widely known to have "spread the word."[13]

In the early to mid-1800s, throughout the southern interior of British Columbia, a religious movement known as the "prophet cult" gained numerous native followers. At the centre of this movement was the creator figure, "Chief Above," also known as "Chief of the Dead." Entire communities joined together in the worship of this all-powerful deity, under the leadership of a man or woman considered to be a visionary or a prophet because he or she could communicate with this deity. Occasionally these prophets died and shortly afterwards were reborn and returned to life. While dead, they received messages from the Chief Above in the form of songs. Many believed that by dancing and singing in a special manner they would hasten the much hoped for destruction of the world. There was a belief central to this religious movement that the end of the world would terminate suffering, bring happiness and reunite all with their dead relatives.[14]

Some Christian elements were observed in the prophet ceremony—prayer on bent knee, the making of the sign of the cross, and the singing of religious songs.[15] Teit was told that one prophet from the Thompson area travelled throughout the Similkameen Valley prior to 1850 conveying messages about the spiritland and foretelling the coming of the whites and how this would lead to the demise of the Indians. She foretold of the evils of white contact and advised returning to the old ways.[16]

The Judeo-Christian God, as the creator and arranger of the world, appears in other early Okanagan ethnographic accounts. James Teit recorded the following in the early 1900s:

"The Okanagon claim that the earth was made by the "father mystery" or "great mystery"—a mysterious power with masculine attributes, who seems to be the same personage as the "Old One" or "Ancient One" of mythology. When he traveled on earth he assumed the form of a venerable-looking old man. Some people say that he was light-skinned and had a long white beard.

11. Robert H. Ruby and John A. Brown, *The Spokane Indians* (Norman: University of Oklahoma Press, 1970): 534.
12. Heron's Fort Coville Journal, (1829-31). Copies by Kittson [April 13/1830 - May 23/1830]. Hudson's Bay Company Archives B.45/a/1.
13. *The Spokane Indians*: 70.
14. In James Teit's ethnography of the Okanagans, ["The Okanagon," in *The Salishan Tribes of the Western Plateaus*. Extract from the forty-fifth *Annual Report of the Bureau of American Ethnology*, Washington, D.C., 1930], he states that the religious dance of the Okagagon "was in every way like that of the Thompson" (292). The religious or prophet dance ceremony is described in some detail in James Teit, "The Thompson Indians of British Columbia" in *Memoir of the American Museum of Natural History*, 1 (4), 1900: 353-354.
15. Walter Cline, "Religion and Worldview": 174.
16. James Teit, "The Okanagon": 292.

This deity was also called "Chief," "Chief Above," "Great Chief," and "Mystery Above." According to some, the power of the "Great Mystery" was everywhere and pervaded everything. Thus he was near and far and all around; but the main source of power came from above . . . . The "Great Mystery" fructified the earth in some way; and from this union sprang the first people and everything on earth that has life. He said everything on earth should be subordinate to the people, and everything would be for their use, as they were his children . . . .[17]

Partway through one early origin story James Teit noted that, "Here my informant narrated the story of the Garden of Eden and the fall of man nearly in the same way as given in the Bible . . . . So much evil prevailed in the world that the Chief sent his son Jesus to set things right. After travelling through the world as a transformer, Jesus was killed by the bad people, who crucified him and he returned to the sky."[18] Walter Cline, after his work among the Okanagans in 1930, had a strong feeling that "God the creator and supreme being, has developed largely under Christian influence" and that "though present in the folklore, it played a very small part in the old religion."[19] Indeed, when Teit questioned the Okanagan Lake people about one segment of their origin story, he was told that, "Maybe the first priests or white people told us this, but some of us believe it now."[20]

Even in Harry's case, it is possible to see how Christian ideas may have been absorbed into the stories he tells. His grandmother, Louise, was his primary source for stories. She had a brother whose brother-in-law accompanied a priest during his travels, cooking for him, packing his belongings and generally looking after him. According to Harry, this priest told his Okanagan companion a lot of things. The priest's stories no doubt got passed along through the family to Harry's grandmother, who in turn conveyed them to Harry.

Coyote: The First Ancestor

In the beginning God created five people. One of these was Coyote. He was the older of a pair of twins and the only successful diver for the grain of sand which eventually expanded to become the Earth. He was also the first ancestor of the Okanagan people.

Coyote, like all the first people, was part animal and part human. One Okanagan storyteller described his first ancestors as having:

> . . . some of the characteristics that animals have now, and in some respects acted like animals. In form, some were like animals, while others more nearly resembled people. Some could fly like birds, and others could swim like

---

17. Ibid: 289-290.
18. James Teit et. al., "Folk-Tales of Salishan and Sahaptin Tribes": 81.
19. Walter Cline, "Religion and Worldview": 167.
20. James Teit et. al., "Folk-Tales of Salishan and Sahaptin Tribes": 84.

fishes. All had great powers, and were more cunning than either animals or people. They were not well balanced. Each had great powers in certain ways, but was weak and helpless in other ways. Thus each was exceedingly wise in some things, and exceedingly foolish in others. They all had the gift of speech. As a rule, they were selfish, and there was much trouble among them. Some were cannibals, and lived by eating one another. Some did this knowingly, while others did it through ignorance. They knew that they had to live by hunting, but did not know which beings were people, and which deer. They thought people were deer, and preyed on them.[21]

The Big Chief gave Coyote great power. When he sought a name for himself, God gave him two choices. He could be "Sweathouse," or he could be "Coyote." He chose to be Coyote, and with his name, he was given the power to do great deeds, such as to rid the world of bad, people-eating monsters. Harry explains this in detail in the stories, "Coyote Receives a Name and Power," and "Coyote Tricks Owl." Coyote also taught the people basic survival techniques. He never had to die, however, for God gave Fox the power to restore Coyote to life whenever he was killed. In "Coyote Disobeys Fox," Harry explains exactly how Fox interacted with Coyote in order to bring him back to life. Even at the end of the mythological age, Coyote did not die.

As well as being the hero of the people, Coyote was full of pranks and capable of incredible cunning. Stories of his sly and manipulative exploits abound, and have led to his place in Okanagan mythology as the central trickster figure. Harry says of him, "Coyote, he was a bad, bad boy!" This side of Coyote is seen in "Coyote Plays a Dirty Trick," a long and well-known story, in which Coyote concocts a devious plan to get rid of his son so he can steal his son's wife.

Coyote as trickster and culture hero is not unique to south central British Columbia. He is found in the mythology of native groups all over the Plateau, the Great Basin, the Plains and central California. Gary Snyder was particularly drawn to Coyote, though he describes him as "really stupid," "kind of bad," "in fact, really awful," and "outrageous."

> Coyote . . . was interesting to me and some of my colleagues because he spoke to us of place, because he clearly belonged to the place and became almost like a guardian, a protector spirit . . . . For me I think the most interesting psychological thing about the trickster, and what drew me to it for my own personal reasons was that there wasn't a clear dualism of good and evil established here, that he clearly manifested benevolence, compassion, help to human beings sometimes, and had a certain dignity; and on other occasions he was the silliest utmost fool; the overriding picture is old Coyote Man, he's just always traveling along, doing the best he can.[22]

---

21. Ibid: 80-81.
22. Gary Snyder, *The Old Ways*: 83-84.

In Harry's story, Coyote is special among the first people created. He was the only successful diver for the grain which was to become the Earth; it was in his hands that the Earth expanded; and,very significantly, unlike the others who had to follow God's instructions second-hand through written instructions, Coyote was guided orally by God himself. And, most importantly, although Coyote could play the utmost prankster, he was never inherently evil.

By way of contrast, the younger twin, who became the first ancestor of the white people, manifests evil from the beginning. He began life by stealing from and lying to God. In fact, the younger twin, says Harry, "was the first to tell a lie."

Twin brothers, one representing one way of life, and one another, is a common element in mythologies throughout the world. Culture heroes in the form of male twins occur in Iroquois, Central Woodlands, Kiowa, Pueblo, Apache (including Navaho), and a few other native North American mythologies. In South American native mythology, twin heroes are among the most important characters. As in Harry's twin story, one twin is usually strong and clever, while the other is weak and stupid. "The twins are not only transformers, but also great culture heroes to whom mankind is much indebted."[23]

Finally, it should be stressed that both the creation and the Coyote stories of Harry's mythology represent the *living* worldview of a native Okanagan storyteller. Harry lives in the 20th century, but he is deeply connected to his people's remote past, and to his own beginnings. There has been no editorializing to eliminate post-contact reworkings in the stories. In fact, it is Harry's contemporary mythologizing—his reworking of his ancient stories to incorporate events of his lifetime—which makes the collection vital.

A good example of Harry's ability to incorporate current events in a meaningful way in his stories is his interpretation of the landing on the moon of the American astronaut, Neil Armstrong. When news of this event reached Harry, it was not surprising to him at all because he knew that Coyote's son had gone there years ago. The white people were naive, he concluded. Armstrong was *not* the first to land on the moon. He had simply followed the path that Coyote's son had learned about long ago, which is recorded in the old story, "Coyote Plays a Dirty Trick." In this story, Harry sees the earth orbit and the moon orbit of the Apollo mission as the two "stopping points" so critical to Coyote's son's return to earth. Harry is clearly seeing the present in terms of the past, and quickly recognizing new information in a body of old recognitions.

It may puzzle some readers that the white man appears in an Okanagan creation myth. Such a devious character might always have been there and may simply have been identified as the white man in the post-contact world. When one appreciates Harry's explanation of the moon landing, the arrival of the white man on native soil many years ago would have created a similar stir. This momentous event required a place in the great order of things. Clearly, one of the first people had to be the ancestor of these newcomers. In Harry's story, it became the twin brother who could lie more easily, and who could read.

---

23. *The Standard Dictionary of Folklore* Vol.2: 1134-1136.

Similar recognitions apply to the rest of this creation story. In Harry's story there are five original ancestors. Two, we already know. The other three, as explained in the myth, are the original ancestors of the three foreign peoples with whom Harry is familiar—the people of Russia, the people of China, and the people of India.

The purist might edit some or all of the "modern contaminants" out of Harry's story, believing these to be tarnished post-contact influences on an otherwise traditional body of knowledge. This is typical of the scientific tendency to crystallize living, evolving oral culture—to transform myth into a static artifact, an "urtext" which contains the purest essence of what, to the Western mind, a native North American culture *is* (was). To do so is to miss the point entirely. In an oral tradition such as Harry's, where nothing is fundamentally new, and where creation is not some moment in the past, but remains present as the wellspring of every act and every experience in the world, the body of what is known is an integral part of creation. Influences on that body of knowledge work forward and backward in time. Just as the old story of Coyote's son's voyage to the moon and back is brought forward to influence Harry's view of Neil Armstrong's journey, so Armstrong's journey to the moon and back subtly alters the "urtext" of Coyote's son's journey.

Two things are strikingly apparent in "Coyote Plays a Dirty Trick." One, it is only of peripheral importance to the story that the place Coyote's son travels to is the moon. Nothing about the place Coyote's son visits is recognizably particular to the moon. Second, the point of the story is not to explain the moon's presence in the sky or the earth's relation to it. It may very well be that in an earlier telling of this story, Coyote's son simply visited an upper world. Similarly, Harry's view that the Apollo mission involved two interim stopping places, *where you could not get out*, works backward in time to explain the two stops Coyote's son makes on his way back down to earth.

This process bears much in common with the once oral traditions of the Western world. The epic of Gilgamesh, the Bible, the Homeric epics, and the Arthurian cycles were all told and retold for hundreds of years before they were recorded in the fixed and standardized form by which they are known today. The Iliad and the Odyssey, for example, were not created by Homer. He was simply the last recorder of the cycle of stories which had been passed on and modified by storytellers for some twenty generations before him. As such, his account included elements of the early creation myths, tales of a golden age before the "human people," as well as events and understandings gleaned from his own time.

Ironically, to crystallize Harry's stories, either on tape or in book form, also fixes these living stories in time. They will now no longer evolve as they have for hundreds of generations. Indeed, this book might be criticized for Homerizing Harry, though in a relatively unfiltered way. But short of retelling them in the native tongue by a taught, living Okanagan storyteller, what alternative do we have today?

THE AGE OF THE HUMAN PEOPLE

All the stories which follow the creation and Coyote stories are what Harry would call *shmee-MA-ee*. The stories in Part Two are pre-contact stories, but stories which took place after the time of the animal-people. People are "human" as we now know them, but they are living in extremely close association with the natural world around them. As Harry explains it, in the beginning, all the people were animal-people. Later, by God's thought, "they come to be human people." But, in the pre-contact native world, animals and Indians are not completely separated because God gave animals:

> the power to tell 'em [Indians] something, to be power man, to be *ha-HA* because he [the Indian] is with the animal in the first place. That's why the Indians got a *shoo-MISH* [guardian spirit] to the animal, but not the *SHA-ma* [white man].

Four of the stories in Part Two illustrate this strong connection between animals and humans. Two of the animals, the grizzly bear and the wolverine, both strong and potentially ferocious animals, appear in the stories as compassionate and benevolent. Much like the animal-people of the early period, the grizzly looks half animal and half human. She talks; she eats Indian food such as dry meat, black moss, white camas, and Saskatoon berries; and she offers help to a man in distress. Similarly, in the wolverine story, this small, stocky, and potentially vicious animal exerts tremendous energy to save a dying man.

To most people who are reared in an urban setting, these are much-feared animals. To the native immersed in stories and experiences such as Harry's, wolverines and grizzlies are to be treated with respect.

Feuding between the Okanagan and Shuswap people is the subject of the stories, "Rescue of a Sister" and "Throwing Spears." According to James Teit, such feuds between these two groups were common around 1700.[24] In both stories, the main characters use their power in ways unimaginable today. In this way they hark back to the earlier world of Coyote and the animal-people. "Rescue of a Sister" has been circulating for some time. A variant of it, entitled "Left-Arm," was published in 1917.[25]

"Prophecy at Lytton," stands apart from the other stories in Part Two. Composed thematically, layer upon layer, it provides an excellent example of how the oral tradition assimilates new ideas and events. There are two primary story-lines within the one longer story. The first is probably very very old: it explains how God introduced newer and better hunting and fishing techniques enabling the people to use the natural world around them as a perpetually renewable resource. In the second, the mysterious old man announces that he is God and he teaches the people how to pray. Before he leaves, he foretells the coming of the white people.

Set within these two themes is a widely known 'moral tale' in which a boy and his grandmother (Thompson Indians from the Lytton area) are abandoned by their

24. James Teit, "The Okanagon": 258.
25. James Teit et. al., "Folk-Tales of Salishan and Sahaptin Tribes": 98.

people because the boy is lazy. Charles Hill-Tout recorded an Okanagan variant of this story in 1911, which he called, "The Lazy Boy."[26] In this 1911 version, a boy is similarly abandoned by his father because of laziness. He is befriended by a grizzly who teaches him how to survive. Unlike Harry's story, however, neither God nor prophecy appear in the 1911 version of the story. In a Raven tale of the Tlingit and Tsimshian, a boy is similarly deserted by his people for eating all their winter provisions.[27]

"Prophecy at Lytton" contains strong Christian references. When the old man ascends to Heaven, he announces the following: "Now I leave. And you going to see me going up. I come from Heaven. I am the Father. I am God." A similar biblical parallel occurs in the story when the old man first meets the woman and her grandson. He tells them to close their eyes and to pray. When they open their eyes, they find their meager quantity of food has been transformed into a large amount of food, much in the same way as in the biblical story of Jesus' distribution of the loaves and fishes to the masses. Similarly, the prophecy of the arrival of the white man and his new ways may have survived from the days of the "prophet cult."

When God departs, he transforms the patchwork quilt which the boy had made from magpie and bluejay skins into a rock to be a permanent marker of this momentous event. The rock became known as the "spotted rock" and the people considered it sacred—an indicator to them of their special relationship with God. When the whites arrived, they buried the rock to keep it hidden from them. In recent years, according to Harry, elders have been content to allow the rock to fade from all memory, even from that of their own young people, rather than to risk having it sold or stolen.

STORIES OF POWER

At the heart of Okanagan traditional religion is the close affinity of each individual to his or her nature helper—*shoo-MISH*, as it is called in Okanagan. Close alliance with one or more of these put one into a powerful state. With a particularly strong *shoo-MISH*, one can cure one's own ailments, and those of others as well. As Harry describes it:

> You got to have power ... At one time, just like school. Nowadays when every child get big enough to go to school, they got to go to school. That way for the Indians long long time ago. Just like a night or even in the daytime and left them someplace. Leave 'em out there alone by himself or herself. Got to be alone. Animal can come to him or her and talk to them and tell them what they got to do after middle age. And that's their power. They give 'em power and tell them what to do ...

---

26. Charles Hill-Tout, "Report on the Ethnology of the Okanagan of British Columbia, an Interior Division of the Salish Stock," Reprinted in Ralph Maud, *The Salish People* (Vancouver, Talonbooks Vol.1, [1911] 1978): 131.

27. Franz Boas, "Introduction," in James Teit, "Traditions of the Thompson River Indians of British Columbia, *Memoirs of the American Folk-Lore Society* Vol. 6, 1898: 5.

Some people, they can be Indian doctor. They can go to work on some people who were sick. And they can go over there to do the work. But some doctors, like a power man or a power woman, can be a power person all right, but they don't work on the sick person. Just for themself, herself, or maybe on his or her own children. They can help them with their power but not the other people.

The *shoo-MISH* have been an important part of Harry's world since childhood. Although he did not acquire his own *shoo-MISH*, he was sent out alone to train as a child. Whenever he could, he attended the all-night annual winter dances where he watched singers and dancers strengthen and validate their nature-helpers. His wife, Matilda, had her own *shoo-MISH* and was strongly connected to the world of Indian power. Whenever they were ill, or undergoing a period of bad luck, both Harry and Matilda turned to Indian doctors.

Harry spent a lot of time explaining the meaning and significance of Indian power to me, often in the form of stories such as those in Part III. He has dozens of tales about encounters with the *shoo-MISH*, and this has been a major part of his life in the Similkameen Valley.

The first two of the five stories in this section are alike in many ways and are also typical of *shoo-MISH* stories in general. Both tell how two children—in one case a girl and in the other a boy—are out alone in some relatively deserted place. Each hears a voice singing, which talks to them and gives them power. Harry includes in each of the two stories a segment illustrating how, as adults, both the boy and girl use this power they received as children.

The story "Indian Doctor" conveys in beautiful detail how a woman, Susan George, first used her power to save a man. Harry knew her and once was present while she worked on a patient. He said that she could suck blood from a wound, and when she spat it out, it was pitch black.

"Two Cranes" and "Breaking Bones" tell of power of a different sort. In "Two Cranes," two men, while hunting, are given the power by two cranes to produce food from nothing. In "Breaking Bones," a man shows how his power can work its way through his body to his hands in a stickgame.

THE AGE OF THE WHITE MAN

The stories in this final section of the book are from the most recent "Age of Transformation," the age of the white man.

The first item, "Fur Traders," is not really a story, but rather a segment from a long discussion on some of the changes that Harry has observed in his time. "Captive in an English Circus," is the only story in the entire collection which has no displays of "power," no transformations, no dying and coming back to life, no spiritual healing by Indian doctors, and no *shoo-MISH*. George Jim, the central character, lives and dies a victim of white man's ways. But there is a larger significance here too, for, with the absence of *shoo-MISH* in this story, we see fully the victimization

26

of a culture which has become powerless. Here there is no magic; the white man has taken it away. The connection with creation is broken; there is no hope.

"To Hell and Back," takes place in 1886 near Spence's Bridge, British Columbia. The thousands of goldminers who launched the gold rush of 1858 had moved on, but some Chinese, Indians, and a few white miners stayed on to continue working the gold bars. Here too, a native man is plunged into a chaotic struggle under the influence of the white presence.

All of these stories describe a much-transformed world from that of the hunting and gathering life of pre-contact times. Ta-POO-low, the central character in "To Hell and Back," is a rancher and with the cash he has stolen from the goldminers he has murdered, he builds a house, barns, fences, and cellars. He raises crops— oats, potatoes, hay, beets, mangolds, raspberries, and rhubarb. He has pigs and horses. He has lots of money—enough to hire men to work for him.

There is a new form of law and order present in the world of these stories. There are policemen with lists of "wanted men," and there are rewards for turning these men in. There is punishment in the form of long prison terms. There is illegal buying and selling of Indians. There is a world war in which everyone, even Charlie Harvie, a "half-breed" from the tiny village of Enderby, takes part. There are murders along the goldmining bars of the Thompson River. There is illegal whiskey circulating in the native fishing camps, which leads to fighting and murdering. And there is white man's piracy in the trading of guns for furs. The influence of Christianity is evident. An Indian doctor follows one person's soul to Shteen (the Devil), where it is deathly hot and where people are being punished for past sins.

But there are also links to the old ways. In "Captive in an English Circus," the Similkameen people of 1886 are fishing salmon as they have been doing since time immemorial at Oroville in the month of August. There is no town there yet, just two or three white households. The people play traditional stickgames in the evenings for amusement. In "To Hell and Back," the people call upon the Indian doctor, who goes to the sweathouse and uses his power to get to the source of the trouble.

Dying and coming to life, integral to the story, "To Hell and Back," was very much a part of the old native way. Coyote could die, but by the action of Fox stepping over him four times, he could be brought back to life. Sometimes Indian doctors could bring a person back to life immediately after death.

The final story in the book is Harry's telling of the well-known European folktale, "Puss in Boots." As Harry explains, "This is white people stories, because I learned this from the white man." One of the early homesteaders in the Similkameen, John Fall Allison, told this story to his son, Bert Allison, and Bert told the story to Harry. Harry's story follows the European version closely, but the setting is unmistakenly the Similkameen ranch country.

Some European versions of this story end with the boy, now a prince, cutting off the head of the cat at the cat's request. Reluctantly, the boy follows the cat's order and the cat suddenly turns into a prince. But Harry's version ends on a different note. The cat tells the boy that after all he has done, he now expects to be treated extremely well. He must be able to live inside, to lie on beds, to sleep on pillows, and he must be fed well. If anyone mistreats him, chases him with a broom, or forces him to live outside, that person will suffer some misfortune.

It is not surprising that this story appealed to Harry. It is an animal story bearing much in common with his own animal stories. Just as Coyote tricks Owl Woman in order to kill her, the cat tricks his adversary. Like the animal-people of Harry's mythology, Puss in Boots can transform itself into other forms at will, such as a lion, a squirrel, and a mouse. The cat is much like the animal-people of Harry's stories too. It displays human characteristics in its attitudes such as its quest for revenge and retribution, and in its physical characteristics. Harry was surprised to see the picture of the cat with boots on displayed on the wrapping of "Puss in Boots" tinned catfood. It was exactly as he thought the cat should look—part man and part cat.

Indeed, it is not surprising that European tales of animals with magic power would appeal to native Okanagan storytellers. There is a difference, however. Whereas the European might regard the animal story of "Puss in Boots" as a quaint and entertaining fairy tale, Harry regards its moral very seriously. Until recently he always kept cats and he treated them royally, referring to them as "the boys." He warned me seriously after telling the story that "as long as you know that [story], you should be good to your cat."

THE EPIC WORLD OF HARRY ROBINSON

Throughout these now more than twelve years I have been privileged to sit at Harry's table and listen to his stories. In this volume, the reader is invited to listen in. In many ways, Harry's world is our own world, relevant to native and non-native alike. From the established epics of King Arthur or Ulysses, to the narrative epics of Harry Robinson, the oral traditions of a community and society living with the land tell us of a common magic contained therein. Knowledge of this magic as lived and recounted by its storytellers and its prophets, is the beat at the heart of a living culture.

Through his grandmother and aunts and uncles, and his own memory, Harry's stories take us way back to a connection with a living past now scarcely found in evidence anymore. Indeed, Harry is a living example of the advice which his friend, the now deceased Thompson Indian doctor, Josephine George, gave her grandson. When he asked how to remember the stories of his people which she had told him, Josephine simply replied, "Write it on your heart."

PART ONE: BEGINNINGS

THE AGE OF THE ANIMAL-PEOPLE

Harry with Margaret Holding, who taught him to read and write in English.
Photo taken in Omak, Washington, 1922.

The First People

In the beginning, there is nothing but water and darkness. God changes all this by his thoughts, creating the sun, causing a bush to grow up from a vast expanse of water, its blossoms transformed into the first people.

God made the sun.
I said he made the sun,
  but he didn't use any hammer or any knife or anything
    to make the sun.
Just on his thought.
He just think should be sun so he could see.
He just think and it happened that way.
Then after that and he could see.
All water.
Nothing but water.

No trees.
No nothing but sun way up high in the sky.

And God think should be land.
And if it was land, there should be people in the land.
Be better.

So after, he think,
  "I go down and get near to this water
    and see what I'll do."
And he came down on the air.

See?
That was *ha-HA.* *

---

*ha-HA is a native term for which there is no equivalent in English. It connotes a magic power inherent in the objects of nature which is more potent than the natural powers of men. As the anthropologist Franz Boas has explained it, the concept is probably more adequately conveyed in English by the word *wonderful.*

And he came down on the air
  and he get near to the water.
Here's the water right here.
He went down and he just about almost touch the water.
Then he stopped there right on the air.
Nothing to hang on.
Nothing to put his feet on.
Nothing.
Just on the air.
But where's the air?
You can't see the air.

Then he think
  "Should be three little brush to grow
    from the water, to come out from the surface of the water.
   Then, if they do come out they should have leaves,
    and they should have flowers."
He think.
While he think,
  in the moment, in the second,
    then he see the little tree,
      the little bush
        come through the surface of the water.
Then he could see 'em sticking out from the water like that.
Then he could see the leaves and flowers.*
And he was pretty close but still on the air.

And he think, I pick off the leaves.
The leaves are not big, you know.
About that size.
  Pick off the leaves and put 'em on the water.

So he reach over there
  still on the air,
    pull out the leaves and drop it.
And the leaves, they landed on the surface of the water.
And they were small leaves for a little while.

Then he thinks the leaves should be bigger.
  Should be big enough for six men to stand on, he thought.

---

*In another telling of this story, Harry mentions that this bush is a rose bush which blossoms in the month of May.

And the second he thought,
  and the leaves stretch out itself.
And they were big.
Big enough for six men to stand on.
And thick.
And never got sunk.

All right.
After that,
  himself, he thinks to move and stand on that.
Just the one.
Just himself alone.
But he figures
  should be six men on there.
But he's the first one that stand on there.
After he stand on that,
    then this brush with the flower,
      it was quite close.
See?
These leaves kind of stretch out
  and it's kinda floating on the water,
    on the surface of the water.
Then he was standing on the leaf.
Before, no.
Just on the air.
And he reach to pick up this flower.
Then he take one and put it where he was standing.
And he take another one and another one.
Picked up four.
Leaves was just round,
  kind of round like that.
And there should be four.
It's four.
But one of this four is doubled.
It's doubled like that.
Seems to be like that, you know.
It's doubled, but you could still see the side.
But in another way it looks like four.
But one of them is doubled and that makes five.

So he put them on that leaf where he was standing.

And he wants four only.*
But this is five.

All right.
He think,
   This one that's doubled,
     that could be the twin,
       can be called twin.
   Supposed to be only one.
   In another way he's two.
   But in another way he's one because he's double.
   But these others are separate.
All right.
Figure that out and he say,
   "All right, you guys, get up.
   Come alive."
They all get up.
And when they get up
   they five men because this is double.
And that become two when they get up.
But they twin.
And that's the *SHA-ma** and that's the Indian.
These twin, they brothers.

---

*In another telling of this story, Harry mentions that "everything should be in only four." Such patterns of four are common throughout native North American mythology.

**SHA-ma* is the native word for white man.

34

Earth Diver

So now there are five men standing on four leaves which are floating on the surface of the water. God orders each to dive down into the water and to feel around at the bottom for some dirt. One by one they dive.

So all right.
Now they got five men.
Then they stand on that leaves.
Six man.
They got five and himself.
They got six.
And he said to the oldest one,
　"We want the ground.
　We want the dirt.
　But maybe you dive into the water.
　Dive in and down you go as far as you can go.
　And feel around.
　You might happen to touch something.
　If you do, try to hold 'em.
　Try to get some.
　Then you come back."

The oldest one,
　that would be this one,*
　　dive down and he couldn't find nothing.
And he come back.
He said,
　"No, there is nothing I can find."

All right.
This other one,
　"You dive in."

---

*Harry points to his thumb. (Each of the five men corresponds to each of the five fingers of the hand.)

So he dive, feel around.
Nothing.
Come out.
He said,
    "No, nothing.
      I couldn't find nothing."

Then this one,
    "You dive."
He went down.
Couldn't find nothing.
Come back, the three of them.

So he stood there for a while
    and decided to tell this one.
So he went down and he happen to scratch something.
And he come back.
And he caught the very little small grain.
About this size.
It's very little.
He got that,
    and it got stuck under the fingernails.
He feel around and he got 'em stuck in there.
And he didn't know,
    but he got 'em stuck under the fingernail.
That's the older from the twin.

So he come out and he said,
    "No, I didn't find anything."

All right.
He thought to himself,
    for the younger one just to be satisfied,
      let him go down.
He's not going to find nothing.
But just to be satisfied,
    so he wouldn't be jealous.

This one here, he know that he got 'em.
So he sent this one.
He say,

"You go down."
He dive and come back and said,
  "No."

And he says to this one [the older twin],
  "You got 'em.
   You find 'em."
He said,
  "No."
  "Yeah, you find 'em.
   You did.
   You find 'em.
   Let's see your hand."
He says,
  "Put your hand this way like that."
Then he took the little grain out of the fingernails.
And he dropped it in his hand right there.

But I do not know for sure if it's on the left hand
   or if it's on the right hand.
Could be on the right hand.
And he could see a little wee stone, a little grain,
   a little rock, just small.
It come off from the fingernail and on his hand.
Says,
  "You just hold it that way."
And everyone, these others,
   they seen it.
He got 'em.
And the younger one,
   he seen he got 'em.

And that's the one that got 'em.
He said,
  "All right, that's going to be the Earth.
   That's going to be the world.
   And kinda close your hand like that."
And told him not to drop it.
  "Keep it on your hand
     but kinda close your hand."

Close his hand.
And the first thing he know,
  he holding more like a ball.
Big enough, you know.
Just round.
More like a ball.
He had 'em on his hand.
All right.
He just hold 'em there.
And that's the same one,
  the little wee one.
That's the one.
Grow up in a second
  and then he hold it more like a ball.
Says,
  "All right, you hold 'em there a little while."
And he hold 'em in a few seconds.
And these others, they seen 'em.
  "All right," he says,
  "Put it down.
   Put it down this place where we're standing.
   Not to drop it.
   Just slow.
   And laid 'em down."
And he did.
At the second he laid 'em down,
  you can see the lightning when it rain.
Quick.
More than a second.
Very fast.
Just like that, and there was the Earth.
Instead of leaves
  and instead of that kind of a little grain,
   they turn into a kind of a ball.
It's all gone,
  but that was a big Earth.
It stretch out to be that big
  in a second or maybe half second.
And they all standing on it.
Then they could see quite a ways.
But no trees, no grass, no nothing.

Just all mud.
It's not muddy for your feet to be sunk in there,
  but it's just all wet, like damp.
So they walked a ways and then they stopped.

Twins: White and Indian

God has four documents containing written instructions for four of the five men he has created. He gives one each to the first three but he has trouble with the twins. God goes away to think about how to resolve this and when he returns he is faced with an even greater problem.

And he says to this one,
  that's the older one,
    and that's the thumb.
He says to Thumb,
  "All right."

And he got the paper.
The paper was fold like that.
Bigger one.
On his thought, you know.
And everything,
  it's writing just like I did here.
This paper, it's all writing.
And he had 'em like that.
And he says to this older one,
  that's the thumb, he says,
  "I'm going to take you,
    and I'm going to throw you in the air.
    And you can go in the air for a long ways
      right on the air.
    And you can go very high.
    And then when you come down,
      you can come down kinda slow.
    And you landed.
    Wherever you landed at anywhere,
      and that's going to be where you going to be.
    And that's going to be your land.

And that's going to be where you going to be.
You going to have increase.
Going to be a lot of people wherever you landed.
And this paper, you take this paper.
You have 'em in your hand.
Then I throw you.
Wherever you landed, that's yours.
Then you open up the paper
    and that'll tell you what you going to do
        from the time you landed in there
            till the end of the world.
It'll tell you what you going to do.
And you got to follow that.
That's in my thought.
I want 'em to be that way."

He took him.
He throw 'em in the air.
He went long ways and he landed.
Then he get up and looked around.
And he still have the paper on his hand.
  "Well," he thought, "This is my land."
That's what he says.
  "And I'm here now."
And that's the Chinese.
That's the Chinese,
He's the thumb.
He's the older one.
All right.
He says to the first finger,
  that's this one,
    same thing.
He says, "I got another paper."
Says,
  "You take this paper and I'm going to throw you
    just like I did with the first one.
  But not the same way.
  In a different direction.
  And wherever you landed,
    and that's going to be yours.
  That's going to be your place."

All right.
He threw him,
Give 'em this paper and told 'em,
  "When you landed, you open this paper,
    and you read it.
   It's all written there.
   That tells you what you going to do
     from now on till the end of the world."

So he went and landed on the ground.
Get up and looked around.
  "This is my land."
That's the Hindu.
He throw 'em a long ways almost right over the world.
But the world is not as big as it is now today
  at that time.

Can you believe that?

Now, that's two.
And then he take the other one.
They tell the same thing,
  and they give 'em the paper
    and tell the same thing
      and throw 'em.

When he landed,
  get up, looked around.
That's the Russia.

That's all.
But these other two, the twin,
  he thought,
    "All right, I make a settle for these three.
     I'll make a settle for these twin,
       but I'm not going to do it now.
     Later on.
     I got to figure out and find out what they should do,
       how it's going to be."

So he told 'em, he said,

"Now you seen your brothers gone,
    the other one and the other one.
  But you're two going to stay right here
    till I go back to where I come.
  And stay over there for three, four days.
  Four days.
  Then I come back.
  And you guys going to stay right here.
  When I come back, I can tell you
    what you going to be and what you going to do.
  And this paper you supposed to have.
  But there's only one.
  But you guys are two.
  You are twin.
  And I put this paper here.
  I put it down in the land right here
    and I go back.
  And you fellas can stay right here.
  When I come back,
    I can tell you what you going to do.
  And we open up this letter.
  And I'll judge both of you."

All right.
He put the paper on the ground,
  well, just because he's God.
And he find a stone.
And he take stone and put the stone on the paper
  so it wouldn't flew away.
It could stay right there.
Put the rock on the paper.
Leave 'em there.
Went up to the Heaven, they call 'em nowadays.
I don't know what they call 'em those days.
But these two still around.
That's supposed to be the twin.
And that's supposed to be the ring finger
  and the smaller finger.
That's two.

All right.

And after awhile and the older one,
  he thought I'm going to take a walk this way.
So he take a walk quite a ways
  and he come back.
Little while and he think,
  I better take a walk a different direction.
  Maybe I'll walk a little more this time,
    a little farther.
He walk and then he went out of sight from his friend.
He went out of the sight.
And he come back.
Then he says to the younger one,
  "Why don't you walk like I do?
  You walk quite a ways and then come back.
  And you walk out of sight.
  And you come back."

All right.
So he take a walk, the younger one.
Then he come back.
Next time he walk again and he go over out of sight.
Then he come back.

Then this older one, he went away,
  and he went out of the sight.
And this younger one, he look at this paper laying there
  with stone on 'em.
He thought,
  "I take this paper and I hide 'em.
  When our man come back, he'll tell us
    whatever he think he's going to tell us."
And he think,
  This paper, he's going to give 'em to my friend
    because he's the older one.
  He's going to get this paper, not me.
  And he's going to be the boss.
  And not me.
  But I take this paper and I hide 'em.
  And when he come he can ask and we can tell 'em,
    We don't know.
    Wind blow.

It mighta blow it away.
All right.
Took the paper, and then he put 'em under his arm like this.
And he got some kind of a clothes, you know.
He tuck it under the arm.
And he hide 'em there.
When their man came back
  and he know.
He know what they're doing.
But when he come back and they both of 'em there.
And he says,
  "Where is that paper?
    I laid 'em right here.
    And what you fellas do with it?"
The older one.
He ask the older one first.
  "I don't know.
    I seen 'em there but I take a walk and come back.
    I didn't know.
    I don't know where it went."
And he ask the younger one.
Says the same thing.
He says,
  "I don't know."
And, he says,
  "I put some stone on 'em,
    and it should not slide away."
The younger one told 'em,
  "Well maybe,
    we walked around, and we run and we play.
  We musta hit that stone with our feet
    and slide off from the paper.
  Then the wind was blowing
    and the wind blowed it, could be."

But he had it here.
God knows.
And that's become tell a lie,
  that younger one.
And that younger one,
  now today, that's the white man.

And the older one, that's me.
That's the Indian.
And that's why the white man,
  they can tell a lie more than the Indian.
But the white man, they got the law.
Then they mention on the law,
  and he says not to tell lie.
Lie is bad.
In the court you take the Bible,
You kiss this Bible to say the true,
  not to tell a lie.
They know that much because they got the law.
But not him.
But the same white man but the others,
  the bunch, that they got a different idea than the other one,
    and they can tell a lie.
It's begin to do that from that time till today.
And now, if the white man tell a lie,
  it don't seems to be bad.
But if the Indian tells a lie,
  that's really bad.
That's what they do.
See?
They build this road in 1929.
Went through the reserve.
And they said to the Indian,
  "We can collect the money from this road
     because the car has got to have a licence.
    They got to pay for the licence.
    They got to have a licence to be on this road.
    That's the only ways we can collect the money from this road.
    Then, when we got the money
       then we'll pay you for your land
        for the road going through."
All right.
The Indians say, "All right."
They write it down.

And when did they pay?
They never paid 'em yet.
They never did pay.

So, this is a government man, they said that.
And the word, that word,
   he was telling lie.
Since 1929,
   and they collect all kinds of money from this road.
But they never pay for it.
Now they going to put another road through here
   on the old railroad track.
And the Indians told 'em,
      "You got to put the money down.
      We got to have the money in our hand before you do the work.
      If not, leave it alone."
That's why they never build a road two years now.
That's just the part I was telling you, this.
Never mind that.

So at that time,
   God knows that younger one had the paper hide.
He know that, but he don't tell 'em.
   "All right," he said,
   "All right you two, you come with me.
   You go this way and we walk a little ways."

So they walk not too far
   and they see the slough.
Slough water.
Not wide.
Could be like from here to that wall.
Just about that wide.
Because the person, you, me, or anybody,
   they can make a long jump,
      and not just stop on the water and get on the other side.
See?
Anybody can jump about that far, you know,
   if they run from the distance.
Then he get to the edge of the water
   and he make a strong or a long jump
      just about that wide, and then stop.
Then he says to this one, to the younger one, he says,
   "I and him, we stand right here.
   But you can walk up a little ways,

47

quite a little ways, about fifty yards,
    or something like that.
And from there you can run.
You can run fast.
You can run all you can.
Run pretty hard.
And then you can stand right there.
And then you go by us,
    but don't step on the water.
Just before you step, but not to put your foot on the water.
Then you can make a long jump.
You can jump all you can.
And when you landed on the other side,
    don't back.
Not to step on the water.
Try to keep that way."

All right.
Him and the older,
    they were standing there.
And this younger one, he went out a ways
    and he running full speed
        and he step on the edge of the water
            and he make a big jump.
And he was pushing so strong that way.
Then he landed.
And he's kinda back,
    back up, like.
And if he do, he can get in the water.
But he just push that way.
Then he landed on his hand.
But that way and he never get in the water.
And then he get up
    because he landed on his hand,
        and then he get up and turn around.

That's the reason why now,
    I see the jumpers, you know,
        they used to play that kind of game.
Anyone, when they jump, landed,
    as soon as they land, then they look back.

48

They always do.
And this man landed over there.
And then he get up and look back.
Nothing he could see.
Nothing but water right over.
Nothing but water.
He couldn't see these other two.
He come running over
  and he come running past that.
He don't see 'em.
And he stand there awhile,
    and he thought was in a bad way.
      Nothing but water.
      And how am I going to get back?
      I was in a bad way.
That's what he thought.

But told him,
  God from there told him,
    "Yeah, you are in a bad way all right.
    But it was your fault.
    You're going to come back here long time from now
      and you got to do your best to come back here.
    That paper, you had it in your arm.
    You hide 'em there.
    And this is the one, it's going to show you how
      you going to make it to get back here.
    But not right away.
    Long time from now.
    When you are there, you're going to make the land pretty.
    You going to make the land good there.
    And you going to be increase.
    But when you come back, a long time from now,
      you going to have a heck of a time.
    You're going to lose a lot of people.
    There's a lot of people
      that's going to be drowned on that water.
    But still you going to make it.
    But you going to have a heck of a time to make it.
    But that paper, it will show you how you going to do it
      to get back here.

But when you get back to this place,
   you going to stay in this place till the end of the world.
And you're going to do good in this place.
You're going to do the work.
Just like you going to split up.
This one is going to stay here in this place.
That's his land.
But now you on the other side.
But you going to come back and live with him
   till the end of the world."
That's what God says to the white man.
And he got the paper,
   then told 'em,
     "That paper, it'll tell you what to do.
     But you have to tell the Indians."
(Well, they don't say 'the Indians.')
      "You have to tell this one about the paper.
     You're the one that's got to tell him all what's on there.
     You have to tell him.
     You have to let him know.
     I suppose to let you know, the both of you,
       but you hide it and you take it.
     All right.
     But when you get back, it'll show you what to do to get back.
     When you get back, you have to show it to him,
       show him what's on that paper."

But he do.
But he don't tell the Indians the whole story.
He hiding some.
He tell all what they can.
It was all right.
He tell the Indians.
And then he show what they could do.
And he could do like they are.
But still he don't tell 'em all.
He hiding some.
That's the stories about.
And then after that, they talk that over the sea.
See?
That man jump over to the other side.

50

And he don't see nothing but water.
That's how, that's when the sea,
   it stretch out to be a big sea just in a second,
      just when he jump.
Turn around and it's already water.

And him and this other one,
   they go for a ways.
Then he stop and he said to this one,
   that's the older one, you know, from the twin.
But the younger from the twin is on the other side already.
So he said to this one,
   "All right, I let you go alone by yourself.
      Then I want to watch you till you go out of sight.
      Out of the sight around the mountain that way.
      Keep going.
      And you can look around.
      You can find something.
      But I can help you.
      I can help you for you to find out what you should do.
      But I may see you maybe a long time from now.
      You going to be increase."

All right.
And he went.
Went out of sight.
Seems to go round the mountain.
And this one goes back to Heaven.

And there's only one.
Again I told you, only one.
Can you figure that out?
When the big flood came, there's only one.
And this time, that's the first.
But this flood is the second time.
Well, can't you see that way?
Because the flood, it's a long time before.
It was a long time after the world was made
   before they had a big flood.
But this one I was telling you now,
   that was when the first beginning.

But that's the same one.
That's Coyote.
That's the one, told him,
    "You go out of the sight
      Then you can find something.
      You can find out what you're going to do.
      But I will help you.
      But you going to be increase.
      And I will see you a long time from now."

He told 'em that.
And Coyote went around the mountain
    and he never seen 'em no more.

□

And Coyote, he's around,
    and he don't seems to know what happened with him.
He forget that.
He don't know.
He know enough to be around
    and find something to eat,
      because that's God's thought.
He can find something.
He can figure out,
    "I'm going to get this and I'm going to eat 'em."
And he do.
But what happens with him and his brother?
He forget.
He don't know.
Not on his mind for a long time till he hear that word.
Above, not far.
And whoever he was saying,
    "The people they going to be gathered at certain place
      the day after tomorrow.
    Then when they all gathered,
      I'm going to give 'em a name to each one."
And that's the time Coyote, he run.
He want to be there first.

Coyote Gets a Name and Power

It is name-giving time, and everyone is supposed to have a name.
Coyote, (well, he's not Coyote yet), wants to be the first to get a name.
So he rushes off to the name-giving place. But, he is so eager to get
there before everyone else, he becomes tired on the way.

At this time Coyote,
  he was around at a certain place
    just by himself.
There's nobody around.
He's alone.
All alone.
And he heard somebody was talking.
And he was saying
  they want all the people to get together in a certain place.
And he mention the place where,
  but I don't know that where.
He mention the place.
He says,
  "I want all the people to be gathered at that place
    at a certain time."

Coyote hear that, but he never seen 'em.
He looked around everywhere.
And he looked around up in the air.
And he could never see nothing.
But he hear that speak just like nowadays you hear the radio.
That's supposed to be on the air.
Well Coyote didn't hear that on the air.
That's how they got the radio nowadays.
From that time when it begin to get started.
It takes a long time to have a radio now,
  but it's not exactly like Coyote,
    but that was the same.

53

So Coyote, he hear that stories.
And this, whoever was speaking,
   supposed to be the Creator,
      or the Indians call him the Big Chief.
Could be God, in another way.
But they could never see 'em.
He just mention that on the air.
Then all the animals,
   they all hear that at the same time
      just like Coyote did.
And he was alone, but he hear that.
And the other animals, some of them were alone,
   some of them were together,
      but they hear that the same time as Coyote hear that.
And they know where this place is going to be.
He says he wants all the people
   to be at a certain place
      at a certain time
         so he can give them a name.
Each one of them,
   they're supposed to have a name.
That's what he want to see the people for.
They can be all together at one place.
Then he could give them a name.
Each one, he could tell 'em,
   "This is going to be your name."
Mention the name,
   "and this is yours and yours."
Each one, they'll have a name.

So the people, they hear this name,
   but they don't know yet which one is who.
Like, they hear that Cougar,
   that's a name,
      Cougar and Fox and Wolf and Eagle and Bald Eagle
         and so on.
The names, they know,
   but they don't know which one was Cougar
      or which one was Fox.
They don't know yet.
But this time they're going to find out who is going to be Fox,

54

which one.
They find out.
That's what they got to know.

So, Coyote,
  well, he's not Coyote yet at that time.
He must have different name.
His name, Shim-ee-OW.
That's his name, Shim-ee-OW.
That's Indian word, *shim-ee-OW.*
And the way I always say,
  I don't know what that means.
I don't know which language to call that to be *shim-ee-OW,*
  but that's his name.
At that time he's not Coyote yet.
He's not Shin-KLEEP.
His name was Shim-ee-OW.

But, he hear this mentioned
  that all people got to get a name.
So, Shim-ee-OW, he thinks,
    I shouldn't be Shim-ee-OW.
He figures he can have his name changed.
He thinks,
    I shouldn't be Shim-ee-OW.
    I should be Wolf.
    If I'm not Wolf, I can be Cougar.
    If I'm not Cougar, I can be Fox.
    There's three name.
    Either one of them I like.
    I can have my name
      any of these three.
    I can go over to that place,
      and I'm going to try to get there early,
        early in the morning,
          so I can be there first before the other people come.
    And then I can pick up my name.
    I can tell the Chief I want to be Cougar.
    If he said no,
      well, I can tell him I want to be Wolf.
    If he said no,

I can tell him I want to be Fox.
They should give me one of them anyway
   so I can get ahead of these other people.
  So, I'll try to get there early.

But, it's quite a ways.
So he figures he's going to run.
And he's going to go fast at all time and all night
  so he can get there early.
So anyway, he know the place where,
  but it's quite a ways to go.
So, he run.
He run
  and run
    and run
      till it get dark.
See?
He hear that word in the daytime,
  and he run all day.
In the afternoon maybe,
  or anytime in that day
    when he hear that.
Then he started to go.
Run all day.
The rest of the day, he run all that.
Night come,
  and he run
    and he run
      and he run.
Nearly all night.
Getting to be morning,
  towards morning,
    about two o'clock in the morning,
      maybe three o'clock in the morning,
        something like that.
And he got tired because he run quite a ways.
And he got tired.
So he thought to himself,
  Maybe I should stop and rest for a while.
  I get tired.
  If I stay here for a while,

then I go again,
  I'll get there early enough, he figures.

All right.
He stop and he sat down
  and he lay against the tree.
Big tree.
And he lay against it,
  just like this, you know.
He lay against the tree.
And he thought he wasn't going to sleep.
He thought he's going to sit there just to rest.
But he rest there just a little while
  and in a few minutes he get sleepy.
And by God, he was sitting there,
  and then he drop.
He's going to sleep.
    By God, he thinks to himself,
    I should not sleep.
    If I sleep, I might be overslept.
    Better not sleep.
    Just rest here for a while, then go.

But he was wondering what he should do not to sleep.
Anyway, he feels around.
It was dark, you know.
He feels around
  and he find a little small bush, more like a toothpick.
You know, small little bushes, kinda hard,
  more like a toothpick.
And he broke that into small pieces.
Then he open his eye
  and then he put the stick up here
    and then here to keep his eyes open.
Both of them.
He think that way he keep his eyes open,
  he wouldn't sleep.
Whenever anybody when they sleep,
  they sleep with his eyes closed.
But if he keep it open, he wouldn't sleep.
That's what he thinks.

But he's wrong.

Anyway, he did that and keep his eyes open.
In a little while he went to sleep anyway
    with his eyes open.
But he sleep, but his eyes were still open.
So, he overslept.
He sleep there a long time.

By God,
    he wake up
        and his eyes were sore and dry
            and he get that out.
And his eyes,
    he move them till they get kind of wet.
They're dry, you know,
    because they've been open so long.
And they get sore from the stick,
    from the toothpick.
More like a toothpick.
Small.
And he has to work on his eyes for quite a while
    till they get all right.
Then he look around
    and he see that the sun was way up.
It's kind of late.
He figure he should get to that place early.
    Well, by God, he thought to himself,
    I'll go anyway.
    Maybe I'm late.
    Maybe not.
    Never can tell.
    Maybe the others, they never come yet.

So he started.
He run.
He run the rest of the way
    till he get there.

And this Big Chief,
    he was sitting there.

58

His place was fixed up,
   kind of a cupboard, more like a little shed.
If it rain, he can be under it and never get wet.
The Chief, he was sitting there all by himself.
Nobody there.
Shim-ee-OW get there and he says to the Chief,
   "I get here.
    I want you to give me a name."
   "But," he says,
   "I want to tell you.
    There are three names.
    I want one of them.
    If you can give me one of them, all right."

And the Chief told him,
   "Well, you'll have to tell me which name you want
       and I'll see."
He says to the Chief,
   "I want to be Cougar."
   "No," the Chief says,
   "There was one fella come here
       and I give him that name.
    He was Cougar and he go.
    You're too late for that name."
   "All right," he says,
   "I can be Wolf. How's that?"
And the Chief says,
   "No, there was a guy here before you come,
       and I give him that name
          and he was Wolf and he's gone.
    You're too late for those two names."
So, he says,
   "All right, one more I want.
    I want to be Fox."
   "No," the Chief told him,
   "You're still too late.
    There was a guy here and I give him that name.
    He is Fox and he's gone.
    You're too late for these three names."
So Shim-ee-OW, he was kind of sore.
And the Chief told him,

the Chief says to him,
  "I'll tell you.
    There was two names, two names left.
    All the names I give away.
    They all go, but only two left.
    But you can still pick one of these two,
      just like you do these three.
    But there's only two."

Well Shim-ee-OW, he says,
  "All right.
    You got to tell me which name, who."

The Chief says,
  "The one name can be KWEELSH-tin.
    That's Sweathouse.
    And the other name, it can be Shin-KLEEP.
    That's Coyote.
    That's the two names.
    So you take your choice
      which one you want for your name.
    There's only two left,
      but you not going to have them both.
    You can have only one of them."

So Shim-ee-OW didn't know what to say.
He don't know what to do and what to say.
So the Chief told 'em,
  "All right, I can explain how you're going to be
    if you're KWEELSH-tin,
      that is, if you're Sweathouse.
    And I can explain how you're going to do,
      how you're going to be if you're Shin-KLEEP."
That's Coyote.
  "All right," Shim-ee-OW says, "tell me."
The Chief told 'em,
  "If you take the name of KWEELSH-tin,
    you can be KWEELSH-tin.
    That's the Sweathouse.
    You can be only in the one place at all time,
      close to the water or maybe close to the river, close to a slough,

close to a lake or close to a creek.
You've got to be close to any of these water.
And you can be in the one place at all time.
You don't have to go nowhere.
Stay in the one place.
But the people, the human people,"
  (the Indians call that *shtil-SHKAYL*,
    that means, "come alive," "come alive person,")
"When these come, when you're Sweathouse,
  they can come to you and work on you,
    build a fire and put the stone in the sweathouse,
      and go in there.
And they'll have a song.
And sing the song in the *KWEELSH-tin*.
That's like *in* you, like.
You're the *KWEELSH-tin*.
Then they can tell you what they wish to get.
And whatever they wish, then you can give 'em,
  give 'em what they wish,
    to be lived to get old,
      or they wish to get the food very easy,
        just whatever they wish.
They can tell you that and then you can give 'em.
That's what you going to do.
That's going to be your job.
Not only one, but all Indian, all people,
  they come to you.
As long as they come to you,
  as long as they ask you for their wish,
    then you give them
      unless they ask you for some bad wish,
        to do something bad, to kill somebody or to steal,
        or something bad.
Should not give them that
  because they wish for something bad.
They should not be that way.
But as long as they wish for something good, you give it to 'em,
  or they wish to live for a long time,
    wish to live till they get old,
      all right, you let 'em have that.
And whoever they wish that,

and you let 'em have
   and they live till they get old.
But he's got to die.
Maybe very old,
  maybe not too old,
   but he's got to die.
That's what you got to do if you are KWEELSH-tin.
You can only be in one place.
And that's not very good.
You'll get tired of staying in the one place.
But if you take the name, Shin-KLEEP,
  (well, that's Coyote),
If you take the name Shin-KLEEP,
  you going to be named Shin-KLEEP
   and I can give you power
    and you'll have the power from me.
Then you can go all over the place.
You can walk everywhere.
You can go all over in this island here.
And wherever you was in this island,
  that's your right wherever you are.
And there's a lot of danger,
  a lot of bad animal and monster in the country
   and I want you to get rid of that.
You try to kill 'em.
You kill the monster.
The monster,
  that's the animals they can kill and eat people.
Whenever it's like that,
  you hear somebody tell you
   there was one WAY over there,
    doesn't matter how far,
     you go.
You go till you find 'em.
Then you kill 'em.
And after you kill 'em,
  and judge and tell 'em what you should do,
   and not to kill the people and eat 'em
    and not to do that no more.
But tell 'em what they should do
  when the human people come.

Then you can go to another one.
You hear somebody tell you
   and you could see that in your dream.
You dream when you sleep
   and you dream where that bad one is.
You go over there and get rid of 'em.
No matter how far.
Doesn't matter if it's a long ways,
   you go over there.
And that way you can walk all over this island
   and you have to do that for a long time.
You not going to do that in a few years.
It takes a long time
   and I'll give you the power so you can do it,
      so you can make it.
Some of 'em dangerous.
They'll kill you.
Sometimes they might kill you.
Maybe you can't kill 'em.
They can kill you.
If they kill you,
   the Fox, give him the power.
Whenever you get killed somewhere,
   Fox, he'll know.
He can see.
I give him the power.
He can dream.
He can see that when he's asleep,
   or he can see that at any time when he was walking.
I could send someone or something to tell him.
He could hear that word but may not see.
And find out Coyote is dead.
Find out where
   and he can go over there.
And when he come and find you,
   he can look around
      and find where you're dead.
You lay down.
You're dead.
All your hair come off
   and you're rotten.

63

And your hair is scattered all over
  and your bone will be apart
    and it'll be scattered all over.
Fox, he can get them together.
He can get a stick and get them all together.
Your hair, your bone and everything,
  get them together.
Step over them, step over them, step over them,
  either way four times.
This way, that way, that way, and that way.
You come alive.
Then when you come alive,
  you alive again and you go.
Then Fox, he'll leave you.
Fox he'll go in some other direction.
Then you don't have to be with Fox.
Just all by yourself.
Then you look for another job to do.
Wherever you find 'em, you do the work.
All right," he says,
  the Chief, he says,
    "that's what you're going to do
      if you take the name, Shin-KLEEP.
But, if you take the name, KWEELSH-tin,
  you'll stay in the one place all time.
But, if you Shin-KLEEP,
  I give you the power so you can do a lot of things.
Then, you can walk all over the place,
  you could see a lot of the country,
    and a lot of bad ones, and a lot of good ones,
      you could see a lot of people.
That's all animal."

So, this Chief,
  he want him to do that work anyway
    because he want him.

So, Shim-ee-OW, he says,
  "All right, I'll take that name.
  I can be Shin-KLEEP.

64

All right, he give 'em that name
  and now he become Shin-KLEEP.
But before, his name was Shim-ee-OW.
So they still call him Shim-ee-OW.
Still had that name,
  but anyway, he had that new name, Shin-KLEEP.

And he goes all over
  whenever he hears something, they kills people,
    and he go over there and find 'em.
He find 'em and he fool around
  and he tell 'em a lie or something.
Then he used the power, you know.
He use his power.
Then he killed them.
And when he killed them,
  he judge and he says to them,
    "You not going to be that way
      just the way you do now.
    You not going to be that way at all time.
    When the human people come,
      shtil-SHKAYL, when it come,
        you can be this way.
    You're not going to kill people like the Owl."

65

Coyote Tricks Owl

Owl is bad. He preys on people. So Coyote devises a crafty plan to end Owl's killings.

The Owl is bad.
He kills people.
Owl, he's supposed to be big man.
Big tall man.
And he kills people, that Owl.
He's tall and he got the power,
   that Owl, he got the power
Was a big man.
Tall and long arms.
Big arms.
Big man.
Big person, the Owl was.
Big woman or big man.
And he can kill people.
Kill 'em and eat 'em.
He bad.
And he can turn himself into a bird.
Into an Owl.
But in another way, it's a person.
Big man or big woman.
But he can change himself into Owl.
And that's a bird.
Then sometimes he could change himself or herself
   into a big person
      so he can kill people.

So Coyote find that out.

All right.
He look for Owl.

They call that *sa-NEE-na*.
That's an Indian word, *sa-NEE-na*.

And he look around.
And he going along,
  and he see some people.
And he ask and they tell them,
  "You go that way.
    He was over there.
    And you can find 'em if you go over that way."

So he keep going and get closer.
Finally he find 'em.
And this time
  when he found 'em,
    and he change into Owl.
He was Owl.
He was Owl Woman when he found 'em.

And Coyote, he know.
He's a big man.
Strong man or big woman.
He couldn't kill 'em.
Too strong.
He use his power whenever he met 'em,
  whenever he find 'em.
It can be an Owl.
That way it can kill easy.
So he's smart because he's got the power to use.
So that's why that Owl, she changed herself.
Was a woman.
Changed herself into Owl.
And it was Owl already
  when Coyote met 'em.

And he was going along.
And he see a woman walking along.
And they met together.
And he see this woman.
And Coyote say to that woman,
  "You going along here.

Where are you going?"
So this woman, she said,
  "I'm going along to look for some people.
  I kill 'em and I eat 'em.
  I eat people."
And Coyote says,
  "So do I.
  I do the same.
  That's what I'm looking for."

See?
He tell 'em a lie.
He's got to tell 'em lie,
He's got to tell 'em something.
He got to fool 'em, you know, to kill 'em.
He says,
  "I'm the same.
  I'm looking for some people.
  I eat people too.
  So we both the same.
  We can go together."

So all right.
The Owl Woman, she went along with Coyote.
They both people-eater.
They look for people
  so they could kill 'em and eat 'em.

All right.
They kept a'going,
  and Coyote told 'em,
    "You stop here.
    We stop here.
    Then you build a fire.
    Then we can cook something."

They got something to cook.
  "Then I'm going to look around here.
  I might find some berries.
  If I find something to eat,
    maybe I'll let you know

and then we can both get 'em."
So that's just to fool, you know.

So Owl Woman build a fire.
And Coyote went out.
Get on the other side so she couldn't see him.
And he use his power.
And finally he came back with a person.
Coyote, he use his power,
   then he make a person out of his power.
And while he were out there
   he bring the two girls and two boys,
      just young people.
And he bring 'em
   and he come to Owl Woman
      and he says to Owl Woman,
         "I found these young people over there
            and I see them and tell them to come.
            Come along with me and then we going to be here."
And he says
   "Build a bigger fire,"
      he says to these young people.
   "Gather some wood from long ways,
      and get 'em,
         and make a big fire,
            so we'll have a good light."
It's getting to be dark, you know, at night.
And, he said,
   "We'll cook something.
      Roast 'em on the stick
         and eat that."
I don't know what they cook,
   but anyway they had a meal.
They eat something.
I think it was,
   they used to tell that, but I forget.
Mushroom, I think they get that.
And then they roast 'em on the stick, you know.
They eat that.

Then after supper, they say,

"We are glad to get together.
  Now we're six of us.
  We gonna dance.
  We gonna dance and we sing our song.
  And we gonna dance right around the fire."

So they did after supper and they sing their song.
Coyote sing his song and he dance.
The whole bunch of 'em, you know,
  they dance around the fire.
And keep going.
And Coyote, he change the song.
And he sing another song, a better song.
Then he dance and dance.

And Owl Woman, she was pretty happy.
She like that.
She hear that good song, Coyote's song.
And she stop and Coyote told 'em,
  "You got a song.
    You sing your song, and we dance on your song."

All right.
Owl Woman, she sing her own song.
Dance around.
And again.
And Coyote sing his song.
Owl Woman, she was happy.
Then they dance around
  and again Coyote sing his song.
Then he says to the young people,
  "You go out and find me a stick,
    not too big.
    Kinda long, and kinda fork.
    Fork stick.
    Cut it with a knife."
Coyote, he got a knife.

And Owl Woman tell 'em,
  "What did you want that stick for?"
  "Well," he says,

"When I sing one song I sing
  I gotta have that in my hand.
  That's the way I was.
  It's more like Indian doctor.
  So I gotta have that stick.
  So I got one more song to sing,
    when I get that stick,
      sing that song,
        I have that stick in my hand."

So the young people went out
  and get 'em a stick
    and bring 'em.
They cut 'em and they got a long stick.
Got kinda fork, you know.
Then he had that and he dance around the fire.
And she dance, Owl.
And he kinda pushed her, you know.
Pushed her towards the fire.

And then,
  "Ah," she says,
  "I was so happy, and I danced that way and that way."

She keep doing it for a while.
And one time he know that he just push her.
Push her to the fire.

And then, she fall about halfways.
And then, he get that stick.
And then, he stick her at the back of the head towards the fire
  and he leave her there.

Then he get her burned, you know.
She breathe the fire.
And she burned her face.
He burn her.
They kill her.

See?
He fool 'em around.

And these people they had there,
   that's his power only.
That's not real people.
He just had that so they could help him
   so he could fool that Owl
     to kill her.

So after that these other people,
   they disappeared.
They disappeared on the air.
That's not a real people.
Just himself, you know.
Then he killed the Owl.

In the morning when the fire was all off,
   he gather the bone.
And he get them and pick them up.
Then he get the water,
   and he put water and he wrap 'em on something.
Then he take 'em up to a tree.
He climb on a tree,
   and this is just a bone.
And some of the meat, you know,
   it's been burned.
But it's not all burned.
He get them together
   and he wrap 'em up with something.
And he climb up to a tree.
Then he put 'em up there on the limbs,
   on the forks of the limbs.
He put them there.
Stick 'em there.
Then he come back and he look.
And then he says,
  "Now you're there.
   You not going to kill the people no more.
   When the human people come *shtil-SHKAYL* come,
    You going to be Owl only.
   At night you can be sitting on the limb like that,
    on the tree.
   And you could speak like, at night.

72

Then, if the children,
   the people have the children
      if the children, they were cry,
         maybe one year old, two years old,
            you could tell 'em,
               'Shut up.
               Don't cry.
               You hear that Owl?
               He going to come and get you.'
Then you could speak and the child could hear.
And that's Owl.
Because you're sitting up there
   and you speak,
      'Mmmm Mmmm Mmmm.'
That's the way the Owl speaks at night,
   sitting on the tree.
And the child hear that.
Told 'em.
   'Hear that?
   If you cry all the time,
      he'll come and pick you up,
         kill you.'
And the kid'll be scared,
   quit crying.
You can be used only that way.
You can only scare the kids.
And you can do that at night.
Not only for the kids,
   but once in awhile
      if anybody could hear you,
         you could fly and you sitting on the tree,
            and you could say that at night.
Even in daytime you could say that sometimes.
But most of the time,
   you could do that at night.
And you could scare the kids.
That you're going to do.
No more killing people.
No more eat people."

See?

He judge 'em.
He tell 'em what to do.
And not only that.
There's a lot of these people-killer,
   and people-eater, when he kill 'em,
      he always judge 'em,
         and tell 'em what they should do.

And that's Coyote did that.

Coyote Disobeys Fox

Coyote travels along. He wants to explore as much country as possible. Fox meets up with him and gives precise instructions on the route he must take. Coyote follows it for a while, but then at the last minute opts for a short-cut.

Now, here's another stories.
And this stories,
   that's Old Coyote.
That's no more his son.
Him, the Old Coyote.
He was walking along the shore,
  nice place,
    in the big ocean.
That's way down.
And the ocean, when they have a big wave, you know,
  and the water goes up,
    way out, then back again,
      then up again,
        then when they stop,
          then pretty soon this ground
            was just nice and smooth, you know.
It's like cement.
Nice and smooth.
Because the water goes, and back,
  and then it stop and go like that.
And this edge of the water,
  edge of the lake,
    very wide.
And nice and smooth all along.
That's way down the other side of Mexico.

And Coyote, he was walking along.

And he come to that place.
He come to the edge of the sea,
  that's the Atlantic Ocean.
And he see that nice ground along the water,
  along the edge.
    By God, he thought to himself,
    That was nice.
    I can walk on that nice ground.
And he walk and then he trot.
He trot because the ground was nice and smooth
  and level.
He running there.
  "By God, that was nice!"

So he went for quite a ways.
He run for a long ways.
So he got tired.
It was warm because down in that way
  down in the Mexico, they always warm.

So he got kinda warm.
So he thought to himself,
  I better get out of this place
    and go where they got some kind of a bushes,
      small bushes,
        where there was some shade.
  I can go over there and lay down, stay there,
      maybe just sit there in the shade,
        to cool off.
  Too warm.

He went off of that nice land
  and he come to a bushy land.
Bushes just short.
Sagebrush or something,
  but he got shade.
So Coyote he sat there
  and he lay there awhile.
And Fox, he know Coyote, he's running that way.

And Fox, he went along.

And he went along where that Coyote went,
   and he could see his tracks.

Coyote, he go around here.
He walk on this one.
So he tracked 'em.
He said,
   "I'm going.
   I caught up to 'em.
   When I caught up to 'em,
      I'm going to tell 'em what we're going to do.
   I better find him."
So, he go that way.

Then Coyote stop for a rest.
And Fox went.
And Fox, he got some stuff tied up on his tail.
Something like this.
That's why I had this.*
Little bells.
Whenever I tell that story, I show this one.

And Fox, he had one of those.
Bigger one.
And he make more noise.

It was tied up on his tail.
Close, you know, tied up.
And when he was running on that nice ground,
   you could hear that bell, you know.
Nice sound.
So Coyote was sitting there,
   and he hear something from where he was coming.
My God, it sounds nice.
He listen, and he get up and sit down.
Listen.
Something coming.

Pretty soon he looked that way

---

*Harry points to a leather thong with metal bells attached.

77

and he could see Fox.
    "Here comes Fox.
    My God, what's the matter with Fox?
    What did he have?
    There was some nice sound with him."

Fox kept a'coming and caught up to him
  and,
    "Coyote you're here."
    "Yeah, I'm here.
    I stop here.
    I was taking a rest.
    I was going along this nice ground,
      but I get tired and I rest here."

Fox, he says,
  "I see your track way up.
  And I see your track, you're coming this way.
  And I thought I better come.
  I want to caught up to you.
  I want to see you."

Coyote,
  "All right."
Fox told 'em,
  "You're walking this way.
  And where you going?
  You think, 'Where you going?' "

  "Well," Coyote he says,
  "I'm just going this way.
  I don't know that way,
    but I want to go as far as I can go
      and see what I can see that way."

All right,
  Fox told 'em,
    "You have to go on this side.
    Along the edge of the water,
      you go along quite a ways from here.
    Then you could see the ground

getting smaller and smaller and smaller.
And this lake here,
    getting narrow.
And there was a lake on this side.
And a lake on this side.
And the ground getting narrow and narrow and narrow.
And that's where you want to go.
And you want to go by the narrowest spot.
You could see that.
And you supposed to go by.
From there you can see the country
    getting bigger and bigger and bigger.
WAY big.
If you want to go that way,
    you have to go right around."
And Coyote said,
  "I don't know.
  If I want to go, I go.
  If something not right, I should not go."

Well, Fox told him,
  "I want you to go right around."
  "Well," he said,
  "All right."

But he says to Fox,
  "You better give me that stuff on your tail.
  You give me that.
  If you give me that, I will go around
    just where you tell me.
  I go right around."

Well, Fox told 'em,
  "If I give you that, you might die."
  "Oh, I don't know."

Fox says,
  "I will give you,
    but I tell you what you going to do,
      and you going to do it.
  Don't you do something not right.

79

If you do what I tell you,
  you'll be all right.
You not going to die,
  but you go a long ways.
But you got to go around.
It take you a long time before you come to that narrow spot.
But when you come back to that narrow spot
  and you keep a'coming on that side,
    then you could meet me up this way somewhere.
And then we could make some more work from there.
That way."

Well, Coyote said,
  "All right, you tell me what you think I should do."

Fox told 'em
  "I give you this stuff and tied it to your tail.
  When you go down,
    you come to that place getting
      narrow and narrow and narrow and narrow.
  It's a little ways.
  And don't you go over.
  Don't you think
    I'll take a shortcut.
    Just a little ways.
  Don't do that.
  You have to go right around.
  After you passed that,
    and you could see the country,
      getting bigger and bigger.
  But you got to go around on the same side.
  And you can go way down.
  And the narrowest, they get down like that.
  And it come to the point.
  And don't you make a shortcut.
  You got to go right around the point.
  And then come up on the west side.
  Take you a long time to get back to this place here."

And that's what they call that now,
  the white people, they call that Panama.

That's on the other side of Mexico.
Then from Panama,
   and the South America, they getting big.

And Coyote's supposed to go right around.
And Fox told 'em,
   "That country, way down,
      and they getting narrow and narrow and narrow."

And you know, you see that on the map?
That South America, that pretty sharp, way down to the south,
Coyote's supposed to go right around
   and come right around from the point
      and come up.
That's a long ways.

So all right, Coyote, he says,
   "Okay, you give me that.
      I'll do what you say."

All right.
Fox, he take that off
   and tie 'em to his tail.

Then, he says,
   "When you come back on that side,
      long time,
      you keep going that side on the west side way up.
   We'll met again.
   When we met again,
      from there we can go out in the sea.
   We're going to do some work."

All right.
Coyote went.

By God, when he run on that nice ground
   on the edge of the water, you know,
      by God, that sounds nice.
He running, you know.
That bell, oh boy, he like it.

By God, he keep going and going.
Quite a ways.
Then he could see that getting smaller and smaller.
And he come to the narrowest spot.
Stop there and he look.
He's not far.

    "And Fox was telling me not to go across.
    He wouldn't know.
    I can jump from here.
    I can make a good long jump
      and I'll be landed right on the centre.
    And then from the centre
      I can jump,
        and I'll be on the other side.
    Fox, he wouldn't know.
    To heck with this country!
    Too far.
    I don't want to go that way.
    And when I get on the other side,
      and I go.
    To hell with this!"

So he started.
That was the narrowest spot.
And he jump from this side,
  and he landed right on the centre,
    right in the middle.
Then from there, he jump in the other side,
  near the water.
He made it.
But soon as he landed on the other side
  and he missed his guts and belly and everything.
He missed it.

    "What's the matter?"

He look.
Then he could see just like that stream there
  right from the other side,
    it's all along.

82

And that was his guts!

When he jump, they just come right out.
So he seen that and he just spin around,
    fall and he died.

That's right where that Panama is now.

And Fox, he was way up this way,
    but he know.
He know Coyote, he died.
So he thinks,
    "To heck with him!
    Let him lay there till he get all rot.
    Then I can go and I get him to be alive."

So Fox, he was around somewhere
    and waiting for a long time,
        about a couple of months or so.

So Fox went down and find Coyote.
He's rotten and his hair, they all go to pieces.
And he's scattered all over by wind.
And maybe something,
    raccoon or something,
        they scattered him all over.
The bones are all rotten, you know.

So Fox, he get a stick,
    and he get him all together.
Get 'em in one bunch, all together,
    all he can get there.
But still they got some more small hair along.

So he step over him,
    that way
        and this way
            and that way.
Like twice that way and twice this way.
Four times.

So Coyote, he get up
  and come alive and wake up.
Just like it was sleeping.
And he said to Fox,
  "I was going along here and I get tired.
  And I lay down and I sleep.
  And I was sound asleep when you bother me
    while I was sleeping."

Fox told him,
  "Yeah, you sleeping.
  You think you sleeping.
  You die.
  Look at your hair!
  Still there, some.
  You rotten!
  Then I get you together
    and I step over you
      and you come alive.
  I told you not to jump over,
    not to take a short-cut in this place.
  I did told you that.
  You supposed to go right around.
  But you make a jump and that's why you die."

  "Yeah," he says,
  "Yeah, I do that all right."

Fox told 'em,
  "You come along, and we'll go up there.
  Up to the country up there.
  Towards north.
  When we get far away we got to go out in the sea.
  We going to make some islands along the sea."

Coyote said,
  "All right, but you go.
  And I stay here awhile.
  And you go.
  And I'll stay here awhile.
  And I want to go over there.

84

Then that's where I die.
And I'm going to stay there awhile.
And then I go up.
And I'll caught up to you way up there somewhere."

Coyote Plays a Dirty Trick

*Coyote is living in a camp with a lot of people. Among them is his
son and his family. Coyote takes a fancy to his daughter-in-law and
devises a grand plan to dispose of his son.*

Young Coyote was a full-grown man.
He was the son of Old Coyote.
And he's a full-grown man,
  and he's got a wife already.
He's married.
He's got a woman.

And one day,
  the Old Coyote, that was his dad,
    because they were living together not only with his dad,
      but with some other people.
Lots of 'em.
Lots of people.
And they living together in one camp.

But this time,
  the Young Coyote and his dad, Old Coyote,
    his dad told him,
      told his son, he says to his son,
        "I think you should go up on that tree,
          the bluff, the big bluff."
And then the tree, the fir tree
  was standing right to the edge,
    right at the bottom of the bluff.
And the bluff was straight up, like, you know.
And the tree was standing right along the bluff.
It grow up right along the bluff.
Tall, tall tree.
And Old Coyote, he said to his son,
  "The eagle, he has a nest way up,
    almost the top of that tree.
  That's where it got a nest.

And the eagle, it had some young ones,
    the four of them, young ones.
And now, they getting bigger.
They fatter, getting bigger.
Wouldn't be long and they'll be through.
They'll fly and we can never get 'em.
While they were still at the nest,
    they not fly yet.
But the feathers, they're bigger.
You go up that tree.
You climb on that tree.
You climb till you come to their nest,
    you can see right alongside you.
Then, the tree is pretty close to the bluff.
And right in the bluff it's kind of a pocket in there.
And that's the eagle's nest right there."

Then Coyote says to his son,
    "When you come to their nest on the tree,
        then you could see the nest
            right alongside of you, to your right.
    So all right.
    Then all you gotta do is switch from the tree, to that nest.
    There was quite a place.
    You could stand in there.
    You could get in there and sit there.
    And you pick up this bird, young bird.
    You don't have to kill 'em.
    Just pick 'em up and pull the feathers.
    Pull 'em out from their wings.
    And then the tail feather, pull them out.
    And when you get 'em all pulled out
        from there, from this four,
            there are lots of 'em,
    Not to pull out the short feather, the small one.
    The big ones only.
    That's the newest ones.
    Now they use that for feather hat.
    When you get them out,
        when you come back,
            we can make hat from that.
    Use the feathers."

So, he says,
    "You do that.

The rest of the feather, leave 'em there.
Pretty soon they'll grow some more.
Then we have the feather we want,
   but some more grow,
      and then they'll fly.
And their mother and their dad,
   they're still feeding 'em.
As long as they're there and can't fly,
   they got to feed 'em all the time.
So we better go get the feather.
But you have to climb on that tree."

So the Young Coyote said,
   "All right."

And Coyote, the Old Coyote,
   that tree there wasn't really tree there.
He put that tree there by his power,
   just so that tree,
      it can be close to the bluff,
         right along the bluff.
And the eagle nest's there
   so he can just fool his son to go up on that tree.
Then he put that tree there by his power.
But it looks like a natural tree
   been there for all time.

And he tell his son,
   "You go up on that tree."
He says,
   "You come,
      and we going to step out this way.
   From there you can see the nest
      almost to the top of that tree.
   Then we watch awhile.
   You can see the eagle, the old eagle,
      fly to their young ones and feed 'em."

So they went out.
They walked out a ways and they stopped there.
And they watch.
They look over there,
   and the Young Coyote could see
      kind of a pocket in the bluff
         just almost the top end that tree.

Then later on they could see the old eagle,
   the mother eagle and the dad eagle,
      the both of 'em.
The one of 'em fly.
Pretty soon, the other one.
Then one of 'em go out, the other one go out,
   and Old Coyote tell his son,
      "Look, see the mother eagle and the dad eagle?
      They go over there to feed the young ones.
      You go up on that tree and get this young one
         and pull the feather out.
      And the old eagle, they know.
      They wouldn't go over there while you're there.
      When you get there from there,
         then you can just grab the limbs,
            then you can go on the tree,
               then you come down.
      And after you leave there,
         this eagle, they'll go over there
            and they can feed their young ones
               as long as they're there.
      You see 'em now?"
   "Yeah, I see 'em."
   "You climb."

And he made that eagle by his power.
That's not a real eagle.
All them, the young ones and the old eagle,
   that's not eagle.
He made that off his power,
   the old eagle and the nest and that tree,
      just so he could fool his son to go up on that tree.

So they got another idea,
   kinda bad idea.
But these is stories,
   I just have to tell you right through.

So the Young Coyote think
   That's all right.
   I can climb, and when I come to that nest,
      I can just switch to there,
         then get the feather and jump again to that tree,
            and then come down.
   It look all right.

89

Coyote says to his son,
    "You go up and I stand right here and I watch you.
    I can watch you when you switch from the tree to the bluff.
    I can give you,
        I can use my power so you wouldn't drop,
            so you wouldn't miss your grip.
    I can watch you that way,
        and I'm going to stand right here."

He still tell him a lie,
    but he's going to use his power all right,
        but not that way.
He's going to use it in a different way.

So, the Young Coyote, he go up.
He climb on the tree,
    and he climb.
Kinda stop, and he look, and he getting near.
He could see he not far.
And then he can't look over there all the time.
He look and he climb for quite a ways,
    and then he stop.
Then he look and, by God, he gettin' near.
Little more, then he get there.
He climb.

And Coyote stand at the bottom where his son climb up
    and he make the tree grow.
He know that the tree can go up at all times.
He'll never reach the nest,
    and also, the nest will go up.

And the Young Coyote didn't know that.
He did not know.
So he keep doing that.

And then the Young Coyote climb up,
    and then he see that.
And he think he get there in a little while,
    and he climb and he look again,
        and he seems to be gettin' nearer all the time,
            not too far, but not yet.
He keep climbing and climbing and climbing.
And Old Coyote knowed it was like that.

And the tree grow.
And the bluff was going up.
And pretty soon the Young Coyote,
   he don't see the bluff no more.
He think the fog come.
He couldn't see the nest,
   but he could still see the tree.

And Coyote, by his power, he make something
   he could still climb.
Wouldn't be long, the fog, it'll be going away.
And then he can go to the nest.
He can get near to the nest.

And the Young Coyote kept coming, kept climbing
   for a long time.
And he don't see that bluff no more.
And he just see more like a fog.
And he look down.
Nothing he could see down.
They all just fog.

And finally he come out, but he can see.
It's a ground like this.
And that's where the tree comes out.
And that's the power of Coyote, the Old Coyote.
And he decided he could leave that tree.
Just step from the tree to the ground.
What he found instead of nest, instead of bluff,
   and he kinda leave the tree,
      kinda jumped, just stepped,
         and stepped on the ground,
            after he stepped on the ground, and he make a turn,
               nothing he see where he did come from.
It's on the Earth, just like this.
But he never did see how he did get there,
   where.
He know he was coming on that tree
   and he know he leave the tree,
      but where's the tree?
He never see 'em no more.

They more like all fog.
And it just disappeared!
No more!
And the Young Coyote is up there!

And now, it says,
   I've got the paper written here,
      and it says there on that paper.
It says in 1969 the first man that's on the moon,
   that's Armstrong.
He was the first man on the moon.

But they did not know
   Coyote's son was the first man on the moon!
And Mr. Armstrong was the second man on the moon.
So the Indians know that,
   but the white people do not know what the Indian know.

Not all Indian,
   but some.
So, that's the way that goes.

And Mr. Coyote, the Young Coyote,
   was up to the moon at that time,
      before Armstrong.
See?
Armstrong get up to the moon in '69.
But Coyote's son,
   a long long time before Christ.
Then how long Christ, since he was born?
1981 since he was born.
Then before that he was up to the moon.
And the white people,
   they say he's up to the moon the first man.
But he is not the first man.
Coyote's son was the first man.
So, nobody know that.
Maybe someone know.
Not around here.
Maybe long ways from here.

So Coyote, that's the Young Coyote,
   he walked.
The country, just like this, the Earth,
   but it's nice.

Little different than this, but nice country.
They got some trees,
  and they got some grass,
    and it seems to be kinda soft to walk.
It's not as hard as this ground here.
It's ground, but it seems to be kinda soft.
Sometimes I see that on the mountain,
  way up on the mountain, you know.
Just kind of a moss, like.
They kinda soft.
They like that all over.
Nice walking.
And they got some trees,
  and they got some little mountains,
    very low mountain.
He can see a long way.
He can see long ways everywhere.

And he don't know which way he was going.
He watch.
So he figure,
  he looked around,
    and he think,
      "I go that way.
        Maybe I walk that way for quite a ways and stop.
        Maybe turn and walk that way for a long ways."

And keep turning.
Look around,
  and he forget where he come from.
By Coyote's power,
  the old man's power.

So he walked for quite a ways,
  and then he seems to come out on a little ridge,
    on the mountain.
And he can see a long ways.
And he walk for a long ways,
  and he seems to come out on a little ridge.

Nobody.
No people.
Nothing.
Just a lonely place.
Nothing there.

No deer, no bear, no nothing.
Just himself.

By God, he looked around.
He thinks,
    There's nothing here!
        But it's nice.

So he kept a'walking and a'walking,
    and when the night come, get dark,
        and he stop and sleep.

He never eat nothing.
He never get hungry.

Next morning, daylight,
    and he walk again.
He walk quite a ways and turn and walk that way.
And turn and walk.
And finally he see the smoke come out in a little ridge.
Come to the top.
Then he could see a long ways.
And he see smoke.

    By God, he thought,
    That was a smoke over there!
        Must be someone staying in that place!
        Living there!
        I'm going that way.

So he went.
He walk and walk and walk and walk.
Getting near.
He can still see the smoke.
And the country was just a flat.
No mountain.
Just low.
Maybe little ridge.
Long ways.

And he come to that smoke
    and he could see the teepee.
And that's where the smoke comes,
    out of the teepee.
By God, he thinks,

There is somebody in there!

And he come to the door.
Well, it's not like this, you know,
    the teepee.
They got something flat,
    something flat over it.
That's for the door.

He stood there and he wait for a while.

And whoever was in there, a man and a woman,
    him and his wife, old people,
        very old old man.
And the lady was very old.
And the old man was sitting.
Then he twisting the rope on his lap.
Twisting them.
That's the Indian rope.
They wild rope.
I don't think you ever know that.
There was a few up the road here a ways, not far,
    about half a mile from here
        near the road.
Just growing there.
You could see 'em if you want to see tomorrow.
And that's the stuff they use.
And they give 'em that and they make a rope,
    small rope, about this size.
Maybe a little bigger than this.
But the long one, they make just in one string,
    but long one.
They pile up.
They make that.

And Young Coyote stood at the door,
    wait awhile.
And the old man, he says to his wife,
    "There's somebody at the door.
    Could be some person.
    Maybe we open the door and see."

Old lady told 'em,
    "All right.
    Maybe you can go and open the door and see.

See who's there.
Somebody."

All right.
The old man walk to the door,
    and lift it up.
Turn it this way,
    and there was a boy, man, standing there.
"Well," he says,
"You are a stranger here."
"Yeah."
"All right," he says, "come in."
So, the young man come in,
    and that's Young Coyote.

Tell 'em,
    "You sit there."
The young man sit there awhile
    and the old man told 'em.
Old man, he says to Coyote, to Young Coyote,
    "We never see nobody since we been here.
    We been here when we're very young.
    Our folks, our dad and mom,
        and my wife's people, and my people,
            they lived here.
    And, when we very young and they left,
        and they left us here,
            and they told us,
                'You live here. We go away.'
    And they go away.
    And we don't know which way and where they go.
    We never see 'em no more.
    But we're pretty young.
    And then we're here ever since.
    Now we're getting pretty old
        and we never see nobody.
    You're the first one that we seen
        and we want you to stay here for a while."

The Young Coyote, he said,
    "All right, I can stay here."

Then he stay there,
    and they give him something to eat.
He never eat since he get in that land.

96

He never hungry.
Never eat nothing.
But when they tell 'em,
  "We give you something to eat,"
  "All right," he says, "all right."
Kinda feel hungry then.

So these old people,
  they got food of some kind.
And they give him some food and he eat.

And they tell 'em,
  "You can lay down there."
And they give 'em something to lay down, sleep.

The next day the old man told 'em,
  "You can go out and you can take a walk
    either way you want,
      any way you want.
   You take a walk, long ways, half a day.
   Then you come back.
   And when night comes, then you get here.
   Maybe three or four days like that,
    and maybe we change in some way.
   Maybe we can tell you some different things."

All right.
Young Coyote, the next day comes,
  and he take a walk, a long ways,
   and then he come back.
The next day he went the other way.
On the second day, he take a walk,
  and he was along the place,
   and he see a little brush,
    and he see poplar.
You know the poplar tree?
Poplar.
There was some up there.
But they small.
Not very big.
He see that.
Was a bunch.
He looked at it
  and one of 'em, it was nice and straight.
Not very tall, but it's very nice.

97

He looked.
  "By God, this is a nice tree!"

So he looked the other one.
This other one is not so good.
It don't look so good.
But this one tree,
  it look very nice, pretty.
Then he looked the other one,
  looked back again, was a person.
Turn into a person just like he was!

And he said to him,
  "Hello."

All right.
They talk to one another.
But that was a tree,
  but it turns into a man just like he was.

And then he got a friend.
Now, they two of them.
So they talk to one another.
And Young Coyote, he says,
  "I stayed with that old people over there."
And this other one, he said,
  "I know these people.
  I know they live there.
  I never see them, but I know they over there."

So Young Coyote told 'em,
    "When I come back, you come with me,
      and we going to stay together,
        and then we come together in their place
          and then you see."

All right.
This new man, he went along with Young Coyote
  till he get to the camp,
    to where these old people live.
And these old people,
  the one of them, the old man,
    that was Spider.
Did you know the spider?
There was some spider in this house.

Sometimes they run up in the ceiling.
Then, from the ceiling,
    they come down on the rope and right on the floor.
There's some here but we can't see 'em.
There's so many different kind.
Some of 'em just little,
    but some of 'em bad, poison.
Lot of 'em.

That's Spider.
And that was the one that live there up there in the moon.
Old man,
    but I forget his wife's name.
Could be another Spider.
The both of 'em Spider,
    but one of 'em were a man
        and a woman.

So that's how come and now today
    you can see that spider
        and they can walk on that ceiling.
And his back was down,
    and his legs was up to the ceiling.
And he walk.
He never drop.
But he's upside-down.
Never drop.
Then if he want to come down,
    he got a rope.
But you can't see his rope on his body.
He got a rope, very small.
Sometimes when they're hanging down,
    I could see that.
Easy to broke.
And when he want to come down from up there,
    and he can use that rope.
And he come down on that rope slow, not too fast,
    till he get down.

Before he come down,
    he come to about this far,
        and I kinda scare 'em
            and he go back up on that rope
                but you can never see the rope.

So that's why that Young Coyote,
   he come down the rope from the moon on Spider's rope.
And that's what Spider was making.
Making that rope, a long rope.

And he know, that Young Coyote,
   he's going to get up there.
Then he thinks,
      When he gets up here,
         he can be round here for quite a while
            and I'm going to send him down.
      But I got to put on my rope to get down
         just like I always do.
That's what Spider thinks.

So that's why they're making that rope.
And they're making that rope for many days.
They make long one.
Still making 'em.

And Young Coyote come back with another man.
He found that man.
And he says to Spider,
   "I found this boy and he's my friend
      and I bring 'em here."
Spider says,
   "That's all right.
      All right, that's your friend."
Spider, he says,
   "Maybe you find another one. Maybe, may not."

So the next day, him and that other one,
   Young Coyote and the other one,
      they went out and then they find another one, the same.
That's another poplar tree,
   but it turn into a person.
Then they bring 'em.
That evening when they come,
   there were three of 'em,
      Young Coyote and the two other one.
And Spider, he says,
   "That's all right. That's enough.
      I'm going to send you guys down.
      And these two boys, they got to go with you
         to your country down there.

But not right away.
Got to wait awhile till I finish this rope.
I didn't finish 'em yet."
He says to the boys,
   "Tomorrow you go out and go for walk."
He showed 'em which way to go.
   "You guys can go this way.
   Then while you walking along
      you could find the rope, where they grow.
   Then you get me some,
      all you can get.
   Then bring 'em.
   And then I can use that
      and that'll be the finish.
   And I can finish my work with this rope
      what you going to bring in."

All right.
These boys, next day they walk quite a ways.
And they found a big bunch little bushes about this high.
And it's in a big bunch.
And they get some of that and they broke them out
   and they pull 'em
      and they tie 'em.
One bundle about this big.
And they not heavy, you know.
And the other one.
And they have a big bundle
   and they pack them.
And they get back to the camp.

Said to the Spider,
   "Here's the rope.
   You boys tomorrow, you help me open that.
   We open 'em and get the rope from the outside, you know.
   Get them."
And then he's got to twist that rope
   and fasten 'em to this other one.
So they do that for three or four days.

   "All right," he says,
   "I finish."
He says,
   "Tomorrow I'm going to send you boys down
      to where you belong."

That's Coyote's son, Young Coyote.
   "And these two boys, I want to go with you."

All right.
The next day,
   that's something I just don't know just how it comes.
But anyway, they got the basket,
   the big one,
      because the three men was sitting in there.
That basket was so deep.
And they got the lid on and they big.
It was so big.
And the two men, three men sitting in there.
And then they get some rock.
There was some rock up there,
   that's what they were saying.

They see a lot of rocks up there
   when they were up there, the white people.
And they get some rock, round rock.
So big.
Heavy.
Three of them rock. And they put them in that basket.
And this basket, we seen the picture in this one.
Something like that,
   but only big.
And they put this stone in there, rock,
   round rock, big one.
It's not real round, but it's kind of round.
And they put them in there.
And Spider says,
   "This is for the weight.
    This will take you down because it's heavy.
    It'll go down.
    But it's going to stop twice on the way going.
    And remember," he says to the boys,
   "I let you go down.
    You can sit on this basket with these rocks
       and put the lid on.
    Put the lid on and put 'em tight.
    Then I let you go.
    Let you go down.
    You can feel when the basket goes down.
    And it's going to go down for quite a ways.
    Then it's going to stop.

And it stop in one place.
And not to open the lid, not to look out.
You can open the lid, but don't look out.
Then you can pick one of these stone.
And not to look out.
Not to look around.
But one of 'em can open 'em just so high.
Take one of the stone and put 'em over and throw 'em.
If you throw 'em, never hear nothing.
You can never hear noise or nothing.
Then put the lid back on again.
And all you gotta do is rock.
Rock it. Move it.
Either way, you rock it.
Rock it and rock it.
But you throw 'em, you drop again.
Then you go down about the same way.
You go down for quite a ways
    and stop again same way.
Not open the lid, and not to look around.
Just take the stone and throw 'em,
    and listen awhile.
Don't hear nothing.
Put the lid on just rock and rock.
And down it goes again.
On the third time, stop.
Stop on the third time,
    pick up the rock, one more,
        open it, and throw it.
Listen awhile
    and you can hear the rock hit the ground and roll.
You can heard them rolling.
And then you open the lid.
And you go out
    and that was your country.
And that was your place.
You get down to your home place.
But if you open this and look out,
    first thing you know you'll come right back to here.
That's not the way that I want you to go down."

So he talk to him and him
  and tell 'em all right to get in there
    with the stone with 'em.
And nobody know what Spider do with that,

103

but he let it down.
And these boys,
   they don't see anything open
     or anything like that to where they can go down.
They don't see nothing.
They just like this
   but they get in that basket,
     but they go down.
They can feel.
Go down.
They went down.
Stop.
Open that and one of 'em,
   he stick out his head and look around.
Boom!
In a second, one or two seconds
   he get back to the same place.
And Spider told 'em,
   "I told you not to look."

   "Well," Young Coyote says,
   "This one here, we know that but he look."

   "Now, don't you look again.
   I'm going to send you down again."

They still in there.
And then he go down again.
They go down again and then he stop.
Same way.
And then he take the rock
   and open it so high and then throw the stone.
Listen awhile.
No noise at all,
   so they just move 'em and rock 'em and rock 'em.
Pretty soon they go down.
They go down and they stop at the second time.
Same way.
He take the rock, opened it,
   and the other one went out.
Stick his head out and look.
Pop!
He goes again.
They get back.
Spider told 'em,

"Don't do that.
  Next time you come back here,
    you not going to go down no more,
      and you going to be here the rest of your time.
  Going to be here all time.
  Not to look!
  I want you to get down.
  Don't you look.
  On the third time and that was your place.
  You look around.
  You go out,
    but not on the first and second."

So they give 'em more stone.
Two more.
And then they go down again,
  and they stop.
Then Young Coyote,
  he told the boys not to look.
One of them opens,
  but he says,
    "Don't you stick out."

So he took the stone and threw 'em over.
Don't hear nothing.
And he rock and rock
  and go down again till he stop on the second time.
On the second time, same way.
He watch the boys
  and he throw the one stone over.
Never hear nothing.
He rocky, rocky, rocky.

Then go down again for quite a ways,
  long time
    and then they stop.
Then he open it and then he take the stone
  and never look but he take the stone
    and throw 'em out.
And he could hear the stone hit the ground
  and they roll.
They could hear them rolling like that.
That's the way he was told by Spider.
Then he opens the lid
  and then he goes out.

105

That's this place.
That was in Lytton.
That's in Lytton.
Then Young Coyote, he says,
    "Now this is my country.
      This is my place."
And they come out from that basket.
And Young Coyote, he walk
    and there's supposed to be rock,
        supposed to be bedrock.
Looks like a bedrock.
Flat, right on the ground.
He walk on there.
And now today,
    if anybody know where that is
        they could still see the tracks
            that was marked on the rock.
A few steps,
    maybe three or four steps right on the rock.
And that's Coyote's mark when he come out from the basket,
    the Young Coyote.

And the Indians over there, they know where that is.
Then when they survey the railroad, that CPR,
    and they tell the white man,
        "Looks like your surveying, your line is right on our history.
        We could show you.
        We want you to miss it.
        We want that to be that way all the time."
So they went over there.
They know, the Indians.
They know.
They seen 'em.
But when they get there with the white man,
    they could never see 'em.
They could never see that footmark.
But they know the place.
That was the place all right.
But never could see that footmark.
Just because the white man was with 'em.
Maybe one or two.
Maybe three.
But they told 'em right here.
They told 'em all about it
    and they told 'em just a part of that story.

106

Not all.
Just a part of that story.
And they told the white people,
   "We want you to miss it.
      You can work your surveying from up somewhere,
         and not to hit this part here.
      If you miss 'em, it'll be better."

All right, they do that.
And now today it's still there.
The railroad people, they never fill that.
That's what they were saying.
There was still that place,
   but you can't see the footmark anymore like it used to be.
And some people, one old man,
   he was telling me about it, and he said,
      "Some of them Indian, they went over there
         and they take a good look,
            but they can see very little."
They couldn't hardly see 'em
   since they take the white man over there to show 'em.
Then they couldn't see 'em so good anymore.
But some of them, they could see them,
   but not as plain like it was before.
So that's where Coyote's Son landed.

And now today
   when the white people were trying to get up to the moon
      a few years ago
         and they go on the rocket
            and they went up a lot of times.
They go up, fool around and come down.
And they go up, fool around and go down.
They never get up there for a long time.
There's quite a bunch.
Some of them, they went up from Florida,
   from Germany somewhere,
      go up to the moon.
But some of them they went up so far
   and they watched the speed sign,
      just like the car, you know.
You watch the sign,
   and then, you know, you was on forty miles per hour
      or sixty, the same way.
And they know they were on good many miles,

maybe a thousand miles an hour.
They could see.
They could still see that.
But they find out they was going very slow.
They was so slow they could get out
  and walk around and come in again.
And they was going, but very slow.
But still it shows it's going eight hundred miles an hour
  or something like that, but not in all.
That's just in one spot.
And when he passed that,
  then it goes very fast again.
And he hit that twice
  and some kind of layer between this earth and that other one
    in between the two,
      that's where Coyote's basket stopped.
Then he stop,
  but throw the rock and the rock just drop.
But the basket stop and lay there
  but he could never see nothing.
That's when Coyote come down.

And the same way when the rocket go off.
It goes by these two layers
  and it goes very slow,
    but the register here,
      they could still see going fast but they not going fast.
That's one of them two that seen 'em.
And another one before that,
  before these two,
    two, three men there.
But the other one,
  the first one,
    only one man.
It's different.
Mostly like a plane, what they have.
And they come to the place like that.
We seen that.
It was written in the newspaper
  and they showed it to us whoever they can read.
And he tell me the story.

It's written in newspaper.
That's way back.
You didn't know that.
You not born yet when it happens.
And this man, the first, they try to go up.
They want to know how far they can go up.
And the other man go up and they register, you know.
They can tell how far they went up, how many miles,
    and then come back.
But, the other one,
    who's going to go up the highest they can go?
All right.
They get paid for that if they go up very very high.
When you come back, you get paid.
And this man, there's a bunch of them.
One of them go up,
    maybe two go up, but nothing.
Finally they have to come down.
But one of them,
    there's only one in the plane,
        go up very high.
He can tell on the register.
He was very very high.
He thought he was the highest than any of them go up.
All right.
Stop in one place.
And he think, stop.
He's not moving.
Looked around.
He couldn't see nothing, but he don't go.
Stay.
He know he not moving.
So finally he was setting,
    they small, you know, just for one man.
Finally, he get
    and still hanging on the place
        but he can fall on his feet.
    His feet was on something.
Landed on something like it's standing.
And that's what he says because he writes a letter.
He write all what he seen,

and all what he find out,
   all what he know.
Then somehow he must have carry wood or something.
And he put the paper
   and he wrap it on the wood
      and tie 'em with the strings or the twine.
They tie 'em onto the wood,
   then let it go.
And somehow this wood with the paper on 'em,
   it come right down.
And whoever they are, they find 'em,
   and picked them up
      and take it off from the board and read it.
And that man up there, he wrote that.
And he wrote and he says,
   "I'm here. I stop.
   My machine, it never move.
   It just stop and it stay right here.
   I don't see nothing
      and I try to get out
         and I still hang on to the seat
            but I can feel my feet is on something.
   Feels like I was standing on something.
   So I let the thing go and try to stop.
   And my feet is on something but I couldn't see.
   So I make a walk and I make a circle.
   I walk the circle around, a little ways
      and I walk and come back.
   And I'm going to be here all time
      and I will never get back.
   How can I get back if my thing it's not moving?
   Goodbye.
   I'm going to stay here.
   You can never see me no more."

That's what's on his writing.
And he drop that.
And they found 'em here and they read it.
And where is that man?
Nobody see him since.
He's right. He's still up there.

See?

And that's Coyote's Son,
  he come down
    and stop on that kind of a layer
      and he stop just like that.
Then he rock it and rock it because Spider's power.
Then he drop again.
But this white man,
  his power work,
    and no more power to use
      and he stop and he stay there.
  And he write down
    and I think what he wrote,
      he figure he setting 'em down
        and I think it was go by God's power
          so the other people could see them down there.
That means here.
But him, never did see 'em no more.
So that's the end of that story.

But when Young Coyote get down with these other two,
  and not too long since Young Coyote was down here,
    back to the country.
And these other two, they just disappeared
  and they turn into poplars again,
    just like it was when they were up there.
And that's why they have the poplars now
  any place round in this place.
See? They turn back into poplars again.

But Coyote, kinda bad stories for the Coyote.
Before he went up on that tree
  was sent him by his dad, by Old Coyote,
    and he got a wife and he got a kid, a son.
So he was up there for a while, about over a year.
And the people, they moved from there.
Gee, that's something I forgot to say.
Where the Young Coyote go up on that tree,
  that's from, by God, I forgot that bluff's name.
Anyway, from Oliver off the road

111

there was another creek from the east come down,
   and there was a bluff to your left-hand side
      as the person goes towards Penticton.
Steep bluff.
That's where the Coyote went.
That's the place.
He went up the tree.
And there was people lived there at that time.
Between Coyote landed at Lytton,
  and all these people, they move.
And they lived at Lytton then, when Coyote came down.
And he didn't know where he's going to land when he come.
But he landed over there just where his people was.
  because it was somebody's thought, you know.
And he walked, him and the others, a little ways
Then he could see the little boys,
   the little kids, five or six of them
    they were running around playing.
And they see 'em.
And he was walking kinda slow.
And one of them, he look around
  and he could recognize that was his dad.
And he could see that thing coming down.
The boys watch.
They could see that basket coming down.
And they could see it when it landed,
  but from the distance, quite a ways.
Then they could see these mans coming out and walk that way.
When the mans get near to these kids,
  the kids recognize one of 'em.
That was his dad,
  because they know he went up.
Never come back.
So the boys turn around and run to the camp
  and he get to the camp and he find his mother.
And he says to his mother,
  "We seen something come down from way high
   coming down and landed.
  Big one.
  And the three men went out from there
   and they walk towards us.

And when they get near
   and that was my dad, one of 'em."

And his mother told 'em,
   "Don't you say that.
   Your dad is gone and we'll never see 'em no more."
   "Oh no," he said,
   "He's coming and you'll see him pretty soon.
   He's coming this way."

And Old Coyote, he listen to that boy.
So he knows.
He beat it from there because you know what he did?
When he sends his son off,
   he think that his son,
      he will never see come back.
So he take his son's wife for his wife.
But when he seen his son,
   he heard his son was down, he get home, he beat it.
His son never see him
   and he never see his son,
      but only he hear his grandson.
And his grandson,
   "My dad is coming."
And Coyote, he knows, the Old Coyote.
So he just scram right away.
Away he goes.
Never see 'em no more.
His son never see 'em.
He never seen his son.
So he went the other way,
   and away he goes.
So that's the end of the story.

Coyote is a bad boy, the Old Coyote!

The Flood

Coyote is travelling along, and all of a sudden he hears a voice which carries a very important message for him.

Mr. Coyote was coming along
  right by where Aberdeen is right now.
And he stop and look, and thought to himself,
    At one time I went by this place.
    And now this is the second time I went through here.
    Looks like the water was raising.
    At one time, the first time I go by here,
      and this rock was kind of a ridge.
    A ridge all along.
    But now is all covered with water.
    But only to the upper end.

He could spot that, the upper end.
But before, that's all sticking out along the edge of the water.
Kind of an island quite a ways.
    Looks like the water is raising, he thought.
He kinda surprise, you know.
They went by there a few years before
  and the water was pretty low.
But this time, looks like it was raising.
He think that.
After he think that, and he thought,
  Well, I go.

And he move.
Soon as he started to walk,
  and somebody told 'em,
    somebody told 'em,
      "Coyote, you stop.
        Let me tell you something."

He stop and he hear that voice
  and he looked around.
Don't see no one.
Was wondering why.
And whoever, he told 'em,
  "You just stay there still.
  Don't move.
  Just listen and I'll tell you something.
  You not going to see me.
  Just listen."

Coyote looked around
  and it sounds like it speak
    above his head somewhere this way.
And he looked that way.
Then look around.
Couldn't see nothing.
And told 'em,
  "You're not going to see me,
    but let me tell you something.
  You listen.
  You do what I'm going to tell you."

Well, Coyote just stand still there.
And whoever, he told 'em,
  "Now you think the water was raising.
  It is.
  It's raising all right.
  That going to kill you if you don't watch out,
    if you don't do what I tell you.
  And it's going to kill you.
  They raising all right.
  You can see.
  And you think it was raising.
  And it was raising.
  Now you turn around.
  You can turn to your right
    and go up in the mainland.
  You can go towards northways, like northeast.
  You can go straight ahead to the northeast.
  And you can go not too fast.

But after you go for about halfways
    and you can see the water is going to be behind you.
Water is going to chase you.
Then you can keep a'going.
And you can go way up in the country.
And you can see the country all open.
No nothing.
No mountains.
Just flat.
You can see that.
Then you can see the water
    is going to be right behind you.
Then when you get that far,
    you can see the water's going to be right ahead of you.
And you can see water all over.
But only one place, no water.
You go up there.
You can go up there
    and you can go faster.
When you come to the place
    where there is no water,
        but you can still see the water,
            it come all around.
And it come.
And then you going to be in the water.
But it wouldn't be so deep,
    maybe up to your knees.
But it can be all water.
You can never see no dry land at anywhere.
You could see 'em coming like that.
Soon as you get to that place,
    and the water is going to be up to your knees.
And you just stand in the water there for a while.
Wouldn't be too long and the water go down again.
And then you can see dry land where you was.
Then it's going to keep going down.
Going down, going down."

All right.
Coyote, he turned around to the right.
And seems to be come around to the edge of these

116

lot of lakes.
And he went up towards north.
Towards north like.
Went way, he going fast.
Pretty soon he look back
   and see the water behind him.
   "By God, before I get to the place,
     it going to get up to me."

So he got to speed up
  and keep going
    and running.
Then he could see the country was all open.
No trees, no mountains, no nothing.
Just flat.
But when he get there,
  and then he could he could see the water
    ahead of him.
They're coming.
And behind him.
And water from all over.
And he come on the place where is dry.
Very little.
Nowhere to go anymore.
Stop right there.
Not too long and all covered with water.
And right up to his knees.
And he walked that way a little ways.
And he walk that way.
And just in one place.
Right around.
Water up to here.
That way for so many days,
  and the water went down.
Went down slow.
Went down a little at a time.
And he could see the ground get dry.
But all mud.
All wet.
Went down slow.
Then he get kinda dry.

So he went around.
Walk around.
Pretty soon, they all went down.

And that's when nowadays they call it a world flood.
That's when they had a world flood.
And Coyote is the only one that stands on the world
  when the world was flood.
And Noah and his family
  and the animal, whatever they get 'em in that ark.
That is in the European.
But in this island, nothing but Coyote.
Only the one that stands in this ground when the world flood.
And God's order.
God thought that Coyote's going to be standing up to here.
No more than that.
But the world is covered.
Did you ever hear that stories?
Nobody did, but only one tell me that and I know.
That's the way I heard that.

Coyote Challenges God

*Coyote travels along and meets an old man. He claims he's the older
of the two. The old man invites Coyote into a contest of his power.*

Coyote was walking.
And then he see somebody walking ahead of him.
Looks like this man is walking from here.
And he walks.
And pretty soon they get together.
And they met.
And he looked at him.
He was an old man, a very old man,
  that one he met.
White hair.
Look old.

And he talk to him.
And I do not know for sure what they were saying.
But anyway, they talking to one another.
But Coyote says to him,
  "I'm the oldest.
    You young.
    I'm the oldest."
Coyote, he claims himself, he's older than him.
And this man told him,
  "No, you young.
    I'm the older."
  "Oh no," Coyote says,
  "I'm older.
    I been walking all over the place."

And he tell him all what he have done,
  and explain him how much power he was,
    and so on.

119

But he didn't know he was the one who gave him that power.

So the old man told him,
  "All right, if you got the full power, I like to see."

All right.
They walked a little ways and they see a little mountain.
Not small.
It's kinda big mountain.
He stopped there.
And then this old man told him,
  "If you got the power the way you say,
    a lot of power,
      I want to see you move this mountain
        and put 'em in another place,
          if you got the power."
Coyote says,
  "Why sure, I got the power."
He says,
  "All right.
  I like to see you move that mountain."

So Coyote, he use his power
  and he moved that mountain just by his thought.
And the mountain,
  it seems to move and sit in another place.

All right.
The old man told 'em,
  "All right, you've got the power."
Then they go a little ways and they see a lake.
Pretty good sized lake.
And the old man told 'em,
  "Now you move this lake from that place
    and set it in another place.
    Same as you do that mountain,
      if you got power."
Coyote said,
  "Sure, I'll move 'em."
  "All right, let's see you move it."

So he use his power and he move that lake
  and set it in a different place.
And he told the old man,
  "Now you see, I move it.
    I told you I got the power."

All right.
The old man told 'em,
  "All right, we go back
    and I like to see you move that mountain
      back into place."
Coyote said,
  "All right, I can do it."
So they went back.
And he going to move that mountain.
The old man takes the power away from him.
He didn't know.
He try to move the mountain back to the place.
He couldn't make it.
Can't do it.
Old man told him,
  "All right, we go back to that lake
    and you can move that back in place."
So they went back and he said,
  "All right, you move that back in place."
Try to move but they couldn't move it.
And the old man told 'em,
  "You always say you got a lot of power.
    But you can't move 'em back."
  "Well," he says, "I don't know."
  "Yeah, you don't know but I do.
    I am the one that give you that power in the first place.
    So you used that power
      and you've got the power and you moved that.
    But now I take that power away from you
      for a little while.
    And then you couldn't move it.
    All right.
    Now I give you the power back.
    Then move it."

121

Well, still he didn't know,
   but he get the power back.
Then he moved the lake into place.
And he moved the mountain into place.
Then told him,
   "Now, that's the last thing you can do.
   Now I take the power away from you
      and I'm going to take you
      and I'm going to put you in a certain place
      and you're going to stay there till
         the end of the world.
   Because the reason why I'm going to do that with you,
      you've done a lot of good things
         and you've done a lot of bad things.
   And it seems to be the bad you have done,
      it's more than the good.
   So that's why I'm going to put you in one place.
   And you going to stay there until the end of the world.
   Just before the world is going to be the end,
      I can let you go.
   Then you can go in the place all over again
      just like you do before."

And the old man left him on a boat on the water
   and told him,
      "You're going to be there at all time."

The boat, it goes around itself by wind.
And Coyote stay in there all the time.
For a long time Coyote was there on the water
   sitting on that boat.
And he eat right there.
And he got a fire,
   and the fire never go out.
Just like it was when he first set the fire.
It was like that all the time.
And been there a long time.
Just like he put him in jail.

PART TWO:
THE NATIVE WORLD
THE AGE OF THE HUMAN PEOPLE

Harry with his dog, 1927.

Saved by a Grizzly Bear

Lost and abandoned by his hunting companion, a man wanders into a grizzly's den hoping to die. But a surprise awaits him.

This story I'm going to tell you,
  a man went in the grizzly bear's den
    for spending the winter.
That's the first few words.
But anyway, at one time
  the Blackfoot Indians and the Okanagan Indians,
    the Okanagan Indians used to go to the Blackfoot Indians
      to get the horses.
And this time the bunch of 'em went to see
  if they can get some horses.
They're not buying 'em.
They steal 'em.
The chance they get
  and then they steal the horses.
And this time they went over there,
  not only the two, but a bunch,
    maybe five or six men, maybe more.
They hang around there quite awhile
  but they couldn't get no chance to get horses
    because whoever owns the horses, they watch.
They kinda think,
  the Okanagan Indian they mighta be around there hiding.
They watch the horses.
They got no chance to get horses
  and then they hang around.

So finally, getting to be late in the fall.
Getting late.
And the others, they say,
  "We better go home. We can't get horses."

125

So they left, some of them.
But there was still about three or four more.
But in another week or so
  and the other bunch take off and go home.
But there's two more.
Two man, they still want to get horses
  because if they can get hold of two or three horses,
    they can come home with the horses.
Then it snow.
Getting to be winter.
It might be like in November or December.
So the snow, there's a lot of snow on the mountains.
There's quite a few mountains to go over.
That's likely from Browning, then all the way to Nespelem.
There's a lot of mountains to go over.
When it snowed, then they got some snow on the mountain.
But they still hang around there.
They wanted to get horses.
Otherwise they got to walk on the snow without snowshoes.
So they were there for a while
  but still they couldn't get horses.
And they get hungry.
They got no more food.
So they thought,
  Well, we better go.

Anyhow, they started out from the Blackfoot.
They hiding there all the time.
The Blackfoot, they had an idea somebody been hiding around
  because they might have an idea somehow.
Anyway, they come over.
And they travelled for quite a while
  and then they come to the summit, like.
And the snow is up above the knees,
  something like that.
Then, they got no food,
  and they thought maybe they could get a deer or something
    maybe on the way coming.
But no, there's nothing.
They were hungry.

126

One day they see a bunch of buffalo
  and they sneak up to 'em
    and they sneak
      and only they had is a bow and arrow.
No gun those days.
Not yet.
So they could shoot the buffalo with a bow and arrow.
But they got to get close to 'em if they can, you know.
Otherwise, long distance, they might hit it
  but they wouldn't go in through the skin.
It's got to be kinda close.
So they do the best they can till they get closer.
And one of them,
  he pull the arrow.
Then he shoot the one buffalo.
He hit him right in the rib.
But still he has to run quite a ways and then he falls.
And the others,
  they go away because the buffalo,
    they can run pretty fast and strong.
Anyway, they had one.
And that buffalo is pretty good size, you know.
It was bigger than the cow we seen around here.
So, they got one.
Then, they go over there.
Follow 'em and they find 'em.
He lay there dead.
Then they try to skin 'em
  and then they thought they going to get some wood
    and make a fire,
      and then they going to cut 'em
        and they going to roast 'em.
And so, the other one,
  the one that didn't done the shooting,
    he says,
      "Well, we pretty lucky. We had one buffalo.
        We can dry 'em and we'll have enough food to get home."
And the other one,
  the one that do the shooting, he says to this other one,
    "That's my buffalo.
      You have to shoot your own.

127

        This is mine."
Said,
    "You're not going to get any of 'em."

What do you think of that?
The buffalo is pretty big,
    but he claim it for one man.
That's not good.
So the other one, he kinda mad, you know.
He thought,
    Well, I might as well go
    and see if I can get some of this buffalo.
But he went away, you know.
Seems to go the other direction.
So he went that way.
He thought,
    Maybe I'll go a little ways.
    He might call me back.
Then he walked a ways
    and this one, the one that done the shooting,
        he skin the buffalo
            and he never said nothing to that other one.
He kept a'going and went out of sight
    and try to follow the buffalo that run away.
But they seems to come back the way they come.
That's the way they went, these buffalo.
They can't go that way.
Supposing they go the way they were going,
    he might follow them till he caught up.
He might get one,
    but they went the other way.
So finally he give up.
He thought,
    Well, I better quit and then I'll go home.

So he walked
    and he just go around to that other one and kept a'coming.
And there's a lot of snow.
And this one, the other one,
    he skinned the buffalo
        and cut 'em

and he make a fire and he roast 'em
     so it'll be cooked
     and he dry 'em.
Then he'll have enough.
But he wouldn't pack the whole buffalo
  because there's lots of 'em.
He just cut some of the meat,
  what he can dry and roast 'em
     and then he'll have enough to pack.
Then he'll have enough food till he get home.
But the other one got nothing.

So he went along and he was still mad.
He thought,
   Well, I'm going to die anyway.
   Can't eat.
   Nothing to eat.
   I have to die,
   But maybe I better look for grizzly bear den.
   If I find one, I can go in the den
     and let the grizzly bear kill me.

That's his idea.
So he kept a'going.
Then on the mountains,
  like this, because this is the west
    and this side was facing to the east,
       but this is,
         they got more snow in springtime,
           you know at anytime.
Now the sun goes down
  and they got shade there, but not yet over here.
The place is something like that.
That is where the grizzly got a den always.
And these days,
  the Indian, they say, could see the smoke.
The grizzly bear got a den,
  and the smoke,
     just a small smoke, kind of a narrow,
       but way up, just straight up.
That's supposed to be the grizzly bear's den,

wherever they can see the smoke.
And this man,
  he looked around on the timber like this
    so finally he see smoke,
      just narrow and grey.
So he thought,
  That mighta be the grizzly bear's den.
So he went till he come to it and he find it.
It was a grizzly bear's den.
He could see, you know,
  when the grizzly go in the den
    and he scratch all the grass
      what he can get
        and he pull the grass when he backed in, you know.
He pull the grass
  and he close the door with that grass.
Get tight.
Then the snow come
  and it was covered and he's in there.
So this man, he could see that.
He find 'em
  and he dig the snow
    and he move the snow
      and then he pull that door.
Like, you know, the grass, it was packed in the door.
He pulled that out.
So he go in,
  because he wanted to go in
    so he can get killed by grizzly.
When he go in,
  and he could see there was a fire inside,
    and more like a teepee.
And he got a fire inside
  and the grizzly bear, she was sitting on one side of the fire,
    and she got two cubs.
And these cubs,
  they were sitting on the other side, like,
    and this old bear,
      that would be the mom,
        but it look like kind of a bear or a person.
It's kinda half and half, the way it look like

when this man go in.

So she told him, the grizzly bear told him,
  "You just go over there and sit there."
Says,
  "I'm not going to do anything with you.
  I'm not going to kill you.
  Your idea to come in here so I can kill you,
    but I'm not going to do it.
  I'm going to keep you here for the winter.
  I'm not going to kill you."

Anyway, he sit there
  and the grizzly bear told him,
    "You pretty hungry?"
    "Yeah, I'm hungry."
And the grizzly bear,
  where she was sitting,
    she just move and she just speak there.
Then they get food,
  like the Indian food they use,
    like the dry meat, deer meat, dry meat,
      and black moss and white camas and then saskatoon,
        they all dry.
All the Indians they use,
  they got the same kind of food.
And she get some of that and then she cooked 'em.
Then she give 'em to eat and tell 'em,
  "You stay right there.
  Sometimes if you want to go out,
    I let you out.
  Then for a while you come in again.
  You stay right there.
  That's going to be your home.
  You stay here till springtime.
  I know when the springtime comes.
  And I'll let you know and we can all go out.
  Then you can come with me for a ways
    and then I know where I can show you
      which way to go for you to get home."

Because he's kinda lost, you know.
He doesn't know,
   because the snow, when it come,
      all the country is changed.
They lost at the same time.
He doesn't know which way to go,
   that is, if he keep going.
So anyway, he was there.
And she's got a fire.
And this fire,
   she got no wood there to put some more fire.
This fire, it burning all the time.
They never burn out.
They still going.
There were two poles across the fire
   about this size, a pole.
Then, that's burn and burn all winter.
Towards spring and the grizzly bear told 'em,
   "You watch this fire.
      Whenever it burns and broke in two, the log,
         that means it's springtime down in the lower land.
      But here it's still winter."
Then they were sitting there and sleep.
And once in awhile that grizzly bear,
   she kinda mad and jumped around.
That's where she was and she get mad.
Then she said,
   "Some Indians some place,
      they were saying in the summer
         they going to kill me.
      But I'm going to kill 'em if they try to kill me.
      If they don't get out of my way I will kill 'em."
Sometimes she was sitting there
   and she just laugh and laugh.
Then she said,
   "Some Indian they going to kill me."
But she just say that for fun.
She know she just say that for fun.
She didn't mean it.

So that was all right.

So this man, he hear that.
So they were there till springtime
   and then they could see that wood,
      they were burn, both of 'em logs.
They burn and fall.
But they still burning.
So, the grizzly told 'em,
   "Well, it's pretty near time to go out.
   But wait a little while."
So they wait awhile.
She always feed 'em.
Everyday she cook,
   everyday for that man.
But the grizzly and the cubs, they never eat.
They don't eat anything.
But they got some food just for that man.
She cook food and feed him.
All winter.
Then, she says to that man.
   "Now, we go out. We all go out."
They went out.
They still got some snow but not much.
They went down.
Melt.
So they went down towards the lowland.
Pretty soon they come to a place where there's no snow,
   springtime like now.
So they go a ways and the grizzly bear tell 'em,
   "Did you know, did you recognize this place?"
He said,
   "No. I don't know."
   "All right, then we go a little ways
      and I could show you which way to go."
They went a little ways and stop,
   and tell 'em,
      "You go that way."
She pointed,
   "You go that way.
   Go around the mountain
      and from there and you could recognize the country.
   And you'll know where to get to your home.

All your people is in that camp."
She says, the grizzly bear says to him,
  "When you get back.
    you have to tell 'em that you spent the winter,
      spent the winter in the grizzly bear's den.
    You tell your people,
      but they wouldn't believe you.
    They will never believe you."
But she says,
  "I can give you something
    that can be for your proof
      that you was at the grizzly's den all winter."
  "Well," he says, "all right".

So she give 'em a knife, hunting knife,
  that's not too long.
No gun yet, but still they got knife.
They must have, some people, the Indians,
  they make knife out of the stone, you know.
And she give 'em a knife.
And told 'em,
  "When you get to your home
    and then the people,
      they'll be surprised to see you.
    After a couple of days,
      then you can call the people, all go in one teepee.
    And then you can tell them all about what happens.
    Then when you get through telling 'em
      then you could show them this knife.
    And this man, he could see that knife and he could tell.
    There was one Indian killed by grizzly bear
      about four years ago.
    So, he know that,
      and that was his knife.
    When he was killed with a grizzly bear
      and then the people find that out
        and they went and he was laying there all chewed up.
    He was killed by a grizzly.
    And they know he got a knife
      and they looked around and his knife not there.
    They couldn't find that knife,

134

but the grizzly bear took that knife and keep it.
And this is the knife."

She give it that man for him to show
    that he was in the grizzly bear den.
So this man took the knife.

And this other man,
    when he get home, you know,
        because he got one buffalo to eat all the way home
            then, he got home and the others they tell 'em,
                "Where's your friend?"
He says,
    "He get lost.
    I don't know where he went.
    I kill a buffalo
        and then I just kiddin' him
            and I says,
                'This is not yours.
                This is all mine.
                Maybe you should get your own buffalo.'
    I'm just a kiddin' him
        but he got mad and walked away.
    And I thought maybe he'll come back after awhile,
        but I never seen him since
            and I don't know which way he went.
    He mighta die someplace."

But he's telling lie,
    because he tell his partner,
        "Get out of here. This is my buffalo.
        You have to get your own buffalo."
But he didn't mention that.
He says he's just a kiddin' him.
That's the lie that he say when he come.

So, the first thing they know,
    this other guy, he get home.
In a couple of days, he call the people.
Most of the people go in in one teepee.
And he tell all the stories what happen

135

and he come over and he tell that.
He said,
   "My partner, he shoot a buffalo.
     Then we get there to skin 'em, to cut 'em
       and I was glad, you know.
     But he says,
       'It's not your buffalo.
       This is mine. You have to kill your own.'
     So I thought maybe he didn't mean it.
     Maybe just kiddin' me
       and I went a little ways
        and he don't pay no attention to me.
    And I find, I kinda think
      maybe I should find a grizzly bear den
       and I go in there and they'll kill me
         because I'm going to die anyway.
    Got no food and I can't get food.
  So," he said,
"I find the grizzly bear den
   and I went in, but it's not really grizzly.
It's kind of a half person and half grizzly
   and she talk to me and she tell me all what I think.
And she kept me all winter.
And she feed me.
She got some food.
She feed me all winter.
Then we come out.
I'm still lost and we come out
   and she showed me which way to go to get home.
Then she give me this knife
   for you people, I could show you.
I could show this knife to you people.
Give me this knife.
Remember four years ago the fella got killed by grizzly?"
He mention the certain place.
   "Then he had the knife."
He said,
   "Now, you can get the knife and pass it around."

So, he give the knife the the first one
   and he looked at it.

Well, that was his knife all right,
   the one that got killed by grizzly four years ago.
Then he passed the knife right around.
And this man,
   the one that they tell 'em to
      "Get out of here. This is not your buffalo,"
         he's there.
And then finally the knife,
   he take it right around till it come to that man.
Then this man, he looked at that knife.
Cut his throat with that knife!
Dead!

So, that's the end of that story.
It's kinda hard to believe
   but that's the way I heard 'em
      and a lot of Indians talked about it.

Helped by a Wolverine

At the end of a hunting trip, one man in a party of eight becomes
too ill to make the long trip home. Reluctantly, his companions leave
him behind thinking that he will surely die.

Yeah, these Indians at one time,
  that's quite awhile,
    that was likely before the white people came,
      long time ago.
And they used to go up on that trail from Princeton
  and way up on the mountain that way.
They go out there for hunting.
And a bunch of people, you know.
Maybe ten.
Maybe something like that,
  maybe two bunches.
Maybe one bunch go to some different direction
  and the other bunch go to a different direction.
And this time, this bunch of people,
  could be somewhere around maybe eight,
    and they come from Merritt, that's Thompson people,
      to hunt over there.
It could be in the month of August.
It was in summer.

So they went up and they were hunting for a while,
  camping for a while,
    and they move and they put in a camp.
And they moved around, you know.
That's way up almost the head of Similkameen River.
And one of these mans,
  he got sick.
And he was sick and lay in,
  they make a teepee, you know.

138

And he was sick,
  and he lay there
    and he was sick and sick and sick.
He use medicine.
They make medicine and use that medicine
  but he sick all the time.
He never get better.
And he was there
  and the other ones go out hunting and come back.
He stay in one place.
This man was sick, lay in bed for quite a while.
Then he get worse.
He get weak.
He couldn't walk.
He couldn't get up.
He just lay.

And getting to be late.
Like, could be around in September then already
  or maybe pretty near end of September.
Getting to be kinda late, and they were still there.
Because they got to stay because they can't leave him.
So he getting worse and getting worse.
And they thought,
  well, he said that himself,
    "I think I'm going to die."
So these others,
  they looked at him,
    and they think he going to die all right,
      because he getting thin and getting weak,
        but he still alive and he couldn't move
          and he couldn't walk.
And it getting late,
  and getting cold up there.
So one day he says to this friends,
  this sick man, he says to his friends, he says,
    "I think you guys should move back.
     Move back to our home."
Well, they tell him,
  "Well, what about you?"
  "Well," he says,

"I'm going to die anyway.
 You fellas can go.
 I'll lay right here and I'll die right here.
 Because if you fellas were here, I'll die anyhow.
 Even if you're not here, I'll die anyway.
 So it's too bad for you guys to stay here.
 Getting to be cold.
 You better move back."
He said that to his friends a few times,
  and the others, they think,
    "Well, that's a good idea.
     I guess we have to do that,
        because we can't stay here all the time.
     But he's going to die anyway."

All right.
They tell him,
  "All right, we'll leave you,
    but we going to carry a lot of wood and bring 'em in."
See, the teepee was big
  and they got the fire in the centre
    so the smoke can go right out.
And he was on the one side.
He's got a bed there.
They bring the wood and he broke, you know.
Cut 'em into small pieces.
Not too heavy.
Just light wood.
But they pile 'em on that side of the fireplace
  and they pile 'em.
Lots of wood.
He can get up.
He couldn't walk,
  but he can kinda skid that way
    and he can get some of that wood
      and put 'em on the fire.
Then he could slide back to the bed
  because he couldn't walk.
He couldn't stand up,
  but he could slide, you know.
He could slide.

140

Then they give 'em lot of food
  and he said,
    "Don't give me too much food
      because I'm not hungry.
    I don't eat,
        but just a little bit once in awhile."
Anyway, they give him some food.
That was the deer meat,
  and some other kinds, you know,
    maybe berries, you know.
They give 'em that.
So the others, they pack out.
They pack all their stuff and go.
And that's supposed to go back to Merritt — Shulus.
That's where they from.
So, they left 'em and they say goodbye.
They're gone.
So he's laying there for a while,
  maybe a couple of weeks.
And he's getting worse.
Then he just slide and pick up some wood
  and put 'em on the fire.
And he got a long stick.
And then he move 'em.

Then the, what do you call the, not badger,
wolverine.
That was the animal that could pack anything heavy.
It got the short legs.
I seen 'em.
We killed 'em one time.
It just about this high.
And their legs was short.
And he's kinda wide,
  that wolverine, they call 'em.
They more look like a beaver.
He's kinda wide.
Wide in the back and kinda short legs.
Not too long,
  but it's kinda wide.
It can pack, you know.

I see.
Well, I didn't see.
I saw the track.
It pack the whole sheep.
You know, the sheep was alive.
They got hurt.
They got bit with dog in legs.
Then we make a little corral
   and keep him in there for the time being.
Then I move the camp.
Then whenever I got time,
   I'm going to pack it on the horse
      and take 'em to the camp.
But when I come back he's not there.
And I was wondering how he did get out?
The corral is still there.
Little pen, you know, we make by log.
Then I could see
   it musta drag him under the log
      because the log was so high.
Drag him under the log.
Then I see the tracks of that thing downhill.
Kinda sandy place.
Looks like he was packing 'em.
And I go back to the camp and I tell the sheepherder.
He's older than me.
So he come with me
   and we tracked him quite a ways.
Then we found 'em.
It killed him there and eat 'em.
And I guess it heard us coming
   and and it go away.
It packed 'em long ways.
Could be about mile they packed 'em.
See, the whole sheep, that's heavy, you know.

So, this is the one that come in in his teepee.
And he got a cover on the doorway, you know.
Kinda heavy quilt or something,
   but it come through there.
Then he go over there and he eat his food.

142

He steal the meat, you know,
  and eat them.
And he take some of that and he come out.
Then after awhile he come in again.
Then this man had a long stick
  and he try to scare 'em.
He don't care.
He go over there
  and get the food and go away.
He do that till he pack all the food.
Eat 'em all.
Take 'em away.
He must have a family
  and he take it over there.

And this sick man, he got nothing to eat.
He got lots of wood.
And if it rain or snow,
  he's under the teepee, you know.
He's all right that way.
But nothing to eat
  because his food is taken away by that wolverine.

So one day he thought to himself in the morning,
  he thought,
      I think I better go.
      I go home.
      I go towards home.
Then he try out.
He can go on his hands and knees, you know.
And then how far he have to go in a day?
Maybe couple of hundred yards or more.
Something like that.
So he went.
So he thought to himself,
  I go and I go till I stuck
    and I can't go no more.
  And I'll be dead right there.
  But I go anyway.
So he went.
Started out with his hand and knees.

Go very slow.
In the morning he started
  and he go all day.
And he went,
  could be a mile or something like that
    on his hands and knees.
Then towards evening,
  can be about four o'clock or five, you know,
    getting to be evening.
But he's hungry.
And he wish for something to eat.
He wish.
He said,
  "I wish to have some dry salmon.
    Very good-sized dry salmon.
    That's what I should eat."
He just wish.
But where is he going to get 'em?
How he going to eat that?
But he wish for it anyway.
So he kept a'going.
Then there was a little kind of a hill, you know.
And he come up.
Then he could see from there quite a little ways.
And before he come up
  and he can smell the smoke.
Smells like a smoke, like a fire ahead of him.
And he could see the smoke.
And he think,
  By golly, it mighta be somebody around here.
  Maybe hunting.
  Maybe some people, they might make a fire.
  And maybe the fire is still burning,
    then they might go away.
  If I can get there, might be all right.
  I can be there for the night.
  But I still wish for the dry salmon.

Then he kept a'going
  and kept a'going.
And he get to that smoke.

There was a fire
  and it just getting dark.
Just beginning to get dark.
Get there.
Then he see all the boughs.
They broke the boughs from the tree, you know.
And they laid it on the ground.
Kinda thick, you know.
Looks like it's going to be bedding.
Then he got a big fire and lots of wood piled there.
Looks like somebody were around there but they gone.
The fire was still burning.
And it looks like a bed, you know,
  all the boughs was breaking.
Put 'em up.
And then he could see something near the fire.
And he went over there.
And that was the dry salmon, so big.
Dry salmon.
And he picked it up.
And he broke 'em and eat 'em.
Then after he eat that,
    water's not far from there, the creek,
      just a little ways.
Then he dragged himself over there just a little ways
  and take a drink and come back and lay down.
And it looks like a bed, you know.
Lay down and sleep.

Next morning he wake up
  and the fire was still burning.
Then he put a little more wood.
And he didn't eat 'em all, you know.
Eat some, but he leave some for next morning.
So that morning he eat the rest of 'em
  and he finish.
And away he goes.

He started again early in the morning.
And he keep going.
He know the way, you know.

145

Going towards home.
And he went.
Keep a'going,
  keep a'going, all day.
Towards evening,
  just about the same time, day before,
    and he wished again.
He wish for roast beef,
  I mean, roast deer.
Could be roast rib.
Should be roast on the stick.
That's what they always do.
He wish.
He thought to himself,
  I wish to have some ribs, rib roast for supper.
He wish.
Not too long after that
  and he could see the smoke ahead of 'em.
Then he kept a'going
  and he come to that smoke
    and there was a fire the same way.
There was a fire and lots of wood there.
And there was a bed made there.
And then that roast,
  they have 'em roast on a stick.
And they still on the stick and they stuck it on the ground.
They standing there.
It's just warm.
Close to the fire.
And he pick that up and he eat 'em.
Not very big.
Just small.
Then he eat about half of that and that's enough.
Leave the rest of 'em for morning.
Then, water is not far.
Then he go over there and drink and sleep.

Next day.
He do that every day for a long time.
And then from that place where he start out
  and he kept a'coming.

Come over the hill.
Come over the summit
  and he come down.
Kept a'coming.
And every night he got something to eat.
It was ready before he get there.
Just dark.
Just about dark and then he get there.
And he kept doing that
  till he get to Princeton,
    where town is now
      and where the river meets together
        where the bridge is now.
Because the Tulameen River and the Similkameen River
  meets together.
And that's where they ford, you know, those days.
They forded right at where the river meets.
That's a ford.
And that was in,
  could be around in October already,
    in the fall,
      when he come to that place.
And the same way.
Just before that ford,
  and there was a fire there.
And he got bedding there,
  and he got something to eat.
Dry salmon or deer meat.
Then he eat that.
And next morning,
  then he have to go in the river.
But the river is not deep, you know.
He go on his knees and hands
  and across the river.
He get on the other side,
  and he keep going towards Merritt,
    where the highway is now.
That used to be only trail.
So he went that way
  and the same way all the time.
Everyday, every night.

147

There always be something for him to eat.
And from Princeton,
  he knew how far it was to Merritt.
It's quite a ways and over the mountain too.
And it's just about the same distance from the other way.
Maybe more.
Could be about 150 miles that he go on his knees and hands.
Then he went over the same way everyday.
Get to the summit.
And then he go down towards Merritt.
And when he get so far down,
  and when you go down that road from the summit
    and you go down towards Merritt
      and you see the bunch of poplars on the side of the road.
Down, you know, below from the road in places,
  the poplars, there and there, like a bunch of them.
He come to that place.
Then it was getting to be dark, you know.
Getting late.
He don't see no smoke.
He don't see no nothing.
Getting dark.
But the Indians,
  they live,
    they got a camp right where the town is now.
That's not far from them poplars.
So he stop there for overnight.
He don't see no more.
That's the end.
Every night he always find something to eat,
  but that night he never see nothing.
But he getting close to the people.
So he lay down there and sleep.
Next day he go a little ways,
  little more.
And he pretty sore in the knees and hands.
Then the kids, the little boys, you know,
  the bunch of them,
    then they play.
They running around.
They go up towards the hill, you know.

That way.
Running around.
Play.
And finally they were running
  and they see a man.
He dragging, you know.
Looks more like a bear or something.
They watched him for a while
  and by God, it was a person!
So they go over there.
Getting near.
Then he stop,
  and he sitting down, like.
Then the kids,
  they turn around and run back to the camp
    and tell the rest of the people,
      "We see a man over there.
        He not walking,
          but he dragging.
        He go.
        Looks like he's going on hands and knees."

So the older people, they don't believe that.
Tell them,
  "Oh, you might see some wolverine
    or maybe bear or something."
  "No," they say.
  "He's person.
    He sat down, looking at us.
    We didn't get near because we're scared of 'em."

So finally the older people went over there
  and they seen 'em.
And that was him.
That was the one they left him way back in the mountain.
He was still alive and he was that far.
They talk to him and they say,
  "What's the matter with you?
    How did you get here?"
  "Well, I kept a'coming," he says.
  "I kept a'coming."

But not too long they talk to 'em.
Then he kinda knocked out, you know.
So the Indians, they run back to the camp
   and bring some medicine.
Then they make a fire.
Then they put 'em on the smoke.
And he smoked him all over.
And then he come to again.
And then they put him in the carrier, you know.
They make a carrier
   and then put him in there
      and take him to the camp.
And he get home all right,
   but he's still like that for about another year
      until he begin to get up.
Then he get up
   and he can walk very little, you know.
He walk around.
Another year and he walk around.
He can walk, but not so good.
But he getting a little better all the time.
Pretty soon he getting better and better,
   but not really good.
But he was alive for a long time after that.
But he die.
See?
That's like the end of the stories.
Stop there.

That stories, it come from Merritt.
The people there, long time ago,
   they know that stories and they tell that stories.
And that's how did we hear the stories from there, here.
But now nobody know that but only me.

Rescue of a Sister

*At the upper end of Osoyoos Lake, some Okanagan people have
a camp. One man, Lefty and his younger brother decide to go to
the mountains to hunt deer. The first night away, Lefty has a haun-
ting dream.*

This man, his name, Lefty,
  because he don't use his right hand.
Always use his left.
He's Lefty.
See, that's his name, Lefty.

And he's got a brother.
And Lefty is the oldest.
And his brother was younger than him.

And that's over in Osoyoos Lake,
  in the upper end of Osoyoos Lake.
And that's where the people, the Indians spent their winter
  in that end of that lake,
  in the north end of the lake.
No, they not spend the winter.
They had a camp there anyway
  because the Indians,
    they had a camp in one place for maybe two, three weeks,
     and then they move to another camp.
They keep doing that all summer.
And this time they had a camp there in the summer.
Could be somewhere around in the month of August,
  because they were saying the choke cherries were ripe.
That's the only time the choke cherries were ripe,
  in the month of August.
But anyway, there was a lot of Indians,
  they had a camp there.

Then, this Lefty, he ask some of these Indians there
    so they can go up on the mountains to hunt.
See if they can kill a big deer, big buck, you know.
But nobody seems to wanted to go
    but only him and his brother.
Just the two of 'em.

So, they left from Osoyoos,
    the end of that lake
        and then they go hunting to the west side of that mountain.
So they went up way up to the top
    so they can find a big buck, you know,
        way up on top.
And they get up to the top,
    but it's kinda late in the day, you know,
        getting towards evening.
So they say,
    "We're not going to hunt.
    We just as well stop here.
    And in the morning, early in the morning,
        then we can look around see if we can see some deer."

So, they stop and they make a sweathouse.
They fix up sweathouse, but they never burn 'em.
They wait till morning.
Early in the morning
    then they can burn and go to sweathouse
        before they go out hunting.
So they stop for overnight and go to sleep.
And at night when they were sleeping
    and on his dream it's not good.
There's something happen in the camp.
But he's not sure.
But he's got a bad dream.
So, early in the morning, the next morning,
    just daylight, it was in the summer, you know,
        was pretty early,
            so he tell his partner,
                "We better burn that sweathouse
                    and then we can go to sweathouse."
So they went and they light a fire.

152

Then the fire,
  instead of burn right away, get an awful smoke.
Soon as he see the smoke,
  that's when he find out it was really bad at the camp.
They been killed,
  the people at the camp.
They can find out with his smoke
  but on his dream he's not sure.
There was something happen but he don't know really.
But when he make a smoke, he find out.
So he tell his brother,
  "We should not go to sweathouse.
    We go right now.
    Go down and see what happened.
    Maybe some people from some place come
      and kill our people.
    We might caught up to 'em.
    If we caught up to 'em, we kill 'em."

So they want to fight,
  but just the two of them.
They don't know how many they kill,
  the people down at the camp.
Maybe bunch.

Anyway, they went down.
And they get down,
  down to the camp.
It was a long ways.
In afternoon, sometimes, towards evening
  when they get back to the camp.
And they can see that everybody killed.
They all lay all over.
By God!
Then they looked around for the tracks
  and they seems to go towards east,
    whoever they do the killing.
And they clean up everything, you know,
  food and whatever they got.
They packed them.
That's what they kill 'em for.

Then, he said to his brother,
  "Well we could track these people.
   Some place we caught up to 'em.
   When we caught up to 'em we kill 'em."

And they looked at all the people
  but they missing one.
That was their sister, just a young lady.
She's not there.
She's not killed.
They musta take her along.
They missed her.
But the rest of 'em, they're all there dead.
So he tell his brother,
  "Our sister, she's not in this bunch.
   They must have take her along."

Anyway, they track these,
  that's supposed to be the Shuswap.
They come from Kamloops.
Then they get there and they kill these people.
Then they went towards east and they look for some more.
So Lefty and his brother, they track these.
Track 'em
  and they go towards Rock Creek, that way.
He track them till the night comes and get dark.

And Lefty, he made a cap, a hat.
He make that out of the wolf's head.
Wolf's head, you know.
He skin the head.
Keep the skin, the wolf's head.
Then, the grizzly bear, see,
  he get that out from the head.
And the wolf's skin in the head,
  and the grizzly,
    he sew that together.
Then, he had that for a cap.
And the wolf's nose, it's this way in the front,
  and the grizzly bear's nose is this way.
They was sewed together.

154

That was the skin, you know.
So he had that on.

Then, at night-time they still track the Shuswap.
And his brother told 'em,
  "Maybe we better stop.
    We can track them in the morning when we can see.
    Now it's getting dark and they mighta go somewhere else.
    We mighta go to different direction."
He said,
  "No, I know, because I can smell the tracks.
    I can turn around the grizzly bear's nose
      and I can do better."

So, his cap, you know,
  the wolf's nose is in the front.
But anyway, he turned 'em around.
Then he use the grizzly bear's nose.
Then he smell the track all night.
Then in the morning, the sun was up.
Could be around before noon.
And he caught up to 'em in some kind of a canyon.
Then the Shuswap, they get in the canyon there.
They spent there overnight and they was still there.
Then they come out from,
  see this is a creek, kind of a canyon,
    but not far up the hill and there was a bench there.
When they come there
  and they didn't watch so close
    and they come fast and they come right out at the side.
And the Shuswap, one of them or two, they could see
  and then he said,
    "Look at that.
      There was two man sticking out from there!"
And the other ones look.
They see there but they wolf.
Two wolf.
So they sat there and look for a while.
Two wolf.
And they turned around
  and they packed their arrows, you know,

the bow and arrow,
    and they pack them and they have them in kinda,
        they made out from the skin.
And the arrows, it's in there.
They stuck them in there and then they pack them.
Then he changed himself into a wolf.
Then he took that and then he slide it that way.
Then he turn around and go up the little ridge.
He goes up that way.
And he's got a tail.
That was his arrow.
He pack that
    but he just slide it and he changes into a wolf.

And then these people
    could see there were two wolf.
One was behind.
And they go up to the ridge.
And he says to the first one that seen that,
    "That's a wolf."
    "No," he says, "there was a man, two man I seen."
    "Oh you! You don't know. Look at that. That's a wolf."

So he changed himself into wolf.
So they went up a ways and they went out of sight.

So the other people, some of them,
    they kind of excited.
They thought, maybe somebody tracked them.
But the other ones, they said,
    "Oh no."
So they stay there and they camp there again.
Or if they move they could follow
    because they're going to kill 'em.
So they hide around and they go back that way
    but they don't let them see 'em.
They hide.
So they watch there for the rest of the day
    till it gets pretty near dark
        and then they thought,
            Well, it looks like they're going to stay there.

156

So they wait.
About middle night or maybe towards morning,
  then they went over there.
When they get down and the Shuswap,
  they lay right in a circle that way,
    and the head that way, like that.
And they right in a circle.
And they step over because they're all asleep
  and they lay right around.
They stepped over the Shuswap, they were still sleeping
  till they come to the centre.
And their sister was right in the centre.
She didn't sleep.
She was awoke.
Soon as the people seen that wolf and she thought,
   That might be my brothers.
She expect 'em and she never goes to sleep.
And she was right in the centre
  because they try to kept her that way.
In another way, she might get away.
That's why they kept her in the centre
  and there's a lot of 'em sleep right around.
But Lefty, he step over these people that's sleeping
  and he come to his sister and tell her,
    "All right, I'll take you.
      We'll step over and we'll get out of the sight.
      And then you can go.
      After you go away, I'm going to kill all these."

They had that spear with the more like a bow and arrow.
Head like an arrow head, but they only big, you know.
They had that.
They got a long handle, could be about six feet.
Big arrow.
Sharp.
They had that because that was glued onto the end of the pole
  about this size, something like shovel handle.
They had that and then they got a bow and arrow.
So when they kill the Shuswap with that,
  they just stuck them in the chest or rib, or anywhere.
They kill them.

All they say, "Ah!"
And that's all.
Dead.

So he take his sister and he tell his brother,
  "You stay right there.
  I step all over these Shuswap.
  I was just right in the centre."
So he get there and he take his sister
  and he step over the Shuswap
    till they get over the side
      and then tell 'em,
  "You go far away and stay there.
  I'm going to kill all these."
So he come back and he tell his brother,
  "All right, you go that way.
  And I go this way.
  All you gotta do is to stuck 'em in the side or anywhere.
  Some of 'em lay on the side.
  Some of 'em lay on his back.
  A good chance to do the work."

So they kill 'em.
They kill the most of 'em,
  but there's only a few, maybe four or five,
    they woke up and they know there was somebody killing 'em.
And they get up and they could see there were two man.
So he says to his brother,
  "That's enough. Let them go.
  We don't have to kill 'em. We leave 'em."
So they run.
Then his brother, they went across that Kettle River.
That river, just about something like this,
  a little bigger than this.
And his brother,
  took his sister and went across the river.
But Lefty, still on this side.
Tried to keep these other Shuswap from following these two.
So finally he see them, they run the other way.
And then he jump in the water.
Finally he jump where it's deep water.

158

Then the water seems to be circle there
  and then I guess there was a kind of pole
    and they still connect to rope or something but it's sharp.
So they swing there.
Then he got a vest, skin,
  and that goes right through under the vest, you know.
And over here and then the water float him away
  and then he spring back.
And he float 'em away and then he spring back.
Then he couldn't get out.
He got no way to get out because in deep water.
The water was circle.
Then he float for quite a ways
  and then he spring back.
So finally he has to say,
  "Well, the frog."
    You could hear 'em, the frog.
  "Hurragh, hurragh," at night, you know, in the evening.
So he say that.
So, his brother say to his sister,
  "That's him. He is the one that turn into a frog."
So they went over there
  and he was there and he couldn't get out.
Float down, then swim back.
Float down and then swim back.
He couldn't get out.
Then he says, "Hurragh, hurragh" so they could heard 'em.
So finally they broke that pole like
  and then he get 'em out.

And these other Shuswap,
  there was about three or four, and they go away.
So they turned around and they followed 'em.
He turn his grizzly bear nose and then he follow that.
It was still dark.
And he follow them for quite a ways
  and then they killed the two of them,
    but there's three left.
There was supposed to be five that got away.
Said, "All right, those three,
  we'll let 'em go so they can tell their people

159

when they get home."
Because they want them to get mad,
   to come and then they could kill 'em.

See?
Lefty is quite a guy.
He turn into a wolf.
Then he turn into frog.
Then he find out what happens by the smoke.
Yeah, he's a power man.
In another way he's a power man.
In another way he's an Indian doctor.
That's how it is.
So that's the end of that.

Throwing Spears

*A party of Shuswaps raid an Okanagan fishing camp near Oroville.
The Okanagans defend themselves well and kill all but two of the
attacking Shuswaps. A chase ensues along the east side of Osoyoos
Lake where the Okanagans spot the men, but their spears have
mysteriously disappeared.*

The Shuswap, they come from Kamloops.
And then they went all the way to Oroville
  because they know the Okanagan Indian
    and some other Indian,
      like from Keller, like from Kettle Falls that way,
        there's a lot of Indians there those days.
And they come down from Oroville.
And these Okanagan Indian go to Oroville
And then some from Penticton Indian,
  they go that way.
That's when they get the salmon.
The certain kind of salmon,
  they come all the way up from Portland.
That's from the ocean all the way on the Columbia River.
And then they come to Brewster.
And that's where the Okanogan River
  gets connected to the Columbia River.
Then some of the salmon goes along on the Columbia River
  as far as Kettle Falls.
And some of the same kind of salmon
  but they come up on the Okanogan River.
Then they come up on the Okanogan River
  and then they come through Oroville.
There was one place there, they can get 'em.
Kinda easy to get 'em.
And they can only get that salmon there
  about a week or ten days.

And then they kept going.
Then they come to Osoyoos Lake
  and then they follow that lake all the way
    till they come to the end of the lake.
Then they follow the Okanogan Falls.
  as far as the Okanogan Falls.
They can never go no more.
That's as far as they can go because that was dam.

And the Shuswap, they know that.
So they thought,
    Maybe the Okanagan Indians
     could be gathered in Oroville by now.
    We can go.
    Then we going to kill 'em.

So that's their idea.
Then they come.
But the Okanagan Indians, they don't know.
They thought everything is all right.
So finally they were still there in Oroville.
They getting the salmon.

One night the Shuswap were there
  and they kill some but they couldn't kill 'em all.
They killed them because they were sleeping.
Then they killed some.
Not many.
Just a few.
Then the Okanagan wake up and they had a fight,
    so finally the Okanagan, they kill the Shuswap
     and they kill the most of 'em.
But they kill the Shuswap and they pretty near finish 'em.
There are only two left.

Then the sun come up.
Gettin' daylight and the sun come up.
Then they kill the most of 'em, all but two.
So they say,
   "Well, we leave 'em.
    Let them go home so they could tell the other Shuswap

       what it's left."
So the other ones, they said,
  "No, we better kill them."
So they, the four Okanagan Indians, they chase these two.
They chase 'em on the east side of Osoyoos Lake.
And they thought they going to kill 'em
  or else they want to caught up to 'em
    and then they're going to take that spear from 'em, you know.
They had that, you know, in their hands.
They chase them, the four Okanagan Indians
  and just only two Shuswap Indians.
And they chase them from Oroville
  along the other side of the lake, on the east side of the lake.
And there was a creek from east that runs into Osoyoos Lake.
That's still in the States.
And that creek, I don't know the name of it in English,
  not very big, but they runs into Osoyoos Lake.
And they comes in the open
  and there was kind of a gully, not so deep,
    maybe as high as this ceiling.
Kind of a cut, you know,
  and that's where the creek were running.
And it's got to go down and go up again.

And they chase these two Shuswap.
It's open country.
No trees, but only in the gully.
There were some bushes there, red willows and cottonwoods,
  and some others, you know, along the creek.
But on the bench it's all open.
And they chase the Shuswap.
They watching 'em.
They had their spears in their hand
  and they running.
And they watch 'em till they go down in the creek.
They go down and cross the creek
  and they go up on the other side.
And these Okanagan Indians,
  they getting close to where they can go down.
But they could see the Shuswap.
They coming out on the other side.

163

They didn't have that spear.
When they get down to the creek
  and they thought maybe they throw 'em
    or stuck 'em under the leaves or something.
Left 'em there.
That's what the Okanagan Indians, they thought.
When they get up on the other side,
  they haven't got 'em.
Anyway, they get down and they looked around.
They don't say nothing.
Then they got up and then they chasing 'em for quite a ways
  and then they tell to one another,
    "There's no use chasing 'em.
    They got nothing to do the fighting.
    Maybe we stop and go back.
    They mighta stuck their spears right there someplace.
    And we could find 'em and we could have 'em.
    Let them go."

And he holler and tell 'em,
  "Stop, we'll talk to you."
I don't know how they understand to one another,
  but that's what I heard.
So they holler and the Shuswap stop
  and they went closer and tell 'em,
    "We not going to kill you.
    We'll let you go.
    But when you get back home,
      you tell the rest of the Shuswap about the Okanagan Indian,
        they were chasing you.
    Kill the most of you.
    You're only the two.
    We let you go."

Because they want 'em to get mad,
  what's left over there,
    to come and then they can kill them too.
Okanagans supposed to be better than the Shuswap.

Anyway, and these Shuswap, they cry and then go.
They got no nothing.

164

Their spear,
  the Okanagan Indians thought they must have left 'em there.
They must have hide 'em.
So they went back to the creek
  and they look all over.
They couldn't find 'em.
But they can see the Shuswap didn't have 'em.
They see they have 'em in their hands
  till they get down to the creek.
When they come out they didn't have 'em,
  but they didn't find 'em in the creek.
Where did they go?
They couldn't find 'em.
But when they come out from the creek,
  was still chasing 'em, but they seems to run faster.
Then the Okanagan Indian, they get behind more.
And then they holler and then stop.
Then they just walk over there
  till they get close to talk to 'em.
Then they turn around and cry and run.
So they couldn't find.
They surprised.
They think they don't know what they do with it.
Anyway, these two Shuswap, they get back to,
    now they call 'em,
      ah, gosh, I know the name, but I forgot.
Not Salmon Arm.
Sicamous.
They come to that, yeah, Sicamous.
I been there but I forgot the name.
The Shuswap, that's where they live
  and they come back.
Came home, the two of 'em.
Then, lots of 'em, the rest of 'em, they're there.
After they come home,
  about three or four days
    and there was a lake and the lake was wide.
And one of these two,
  the one of 'em says to one young man,
    and he tell this young man,
      "You take the canoe. Then you go across this lake.

When you get on the other side,
  then you can go that way."

Like they go from here, and when they get on the other side,
  then he can turn to his right,
    then he can go along the shore.
Not too far from the edge of the water, then he said,
  "You go that way and you watch the hillside.
    You might go a little ways
      and you can see kind of a little bluff, not too high.
    They straight for quite a ways till they hit the water,
      come to the shore.
    But it's from the mountain.
    You see them and you just follow that
      till they come to the water.
    Then you stop there and then you get off.
    Then you look around in that little bluff.
    You might find something.
    Whatever you could find, bring 'em."

They don't tell 'em what he's going to find,
  but he tell 'em,
    "You might find something.
      If you find something, bring 'em."
That's the one of 'em that was chased from Osoyoos.
So this young man, he get on the canoe
  and then he go across.
When he get on the other side
  and then he turn to his right
    and then he go along the shore
      and then he could see just a little bluff, not high,
        but it's stone, kind of a wall
          all the way till he got to the lake.
He watch that and he follow that
  till he comes to the lake and he stop.
Get off the canoe and then he pull the canoe out.
And he looked around.
Not very far, not too far
  and he went around and he see
    that spear is lay against the wall.
Rock wall.

That's the spear that was disappeared at Osoyoos.
When they get down at the creek,
    when they get right in the creek,
        then they throw that spear to Sicamous.
They throw 'em in the air
    and that's where it landed.
And that's where he gets his power
    when he was a boy in the first place.
And that spear, it goes back there.
And he sent this young man to go get 'em.
So this young man he found that, two of them.
So well, he thinks, he says,
    "They tell me, 'Whatever you found, bring 'em.'
    Well, I'll take this."
So he goes back across and he say,
    "This is what I found."
    "Yeah, we throw that from over there and we know it's there.
    We want you to go get 'em."

Is that hard to believe?
Who's going to throw things like that from Osoyoos to Sicamous?
But that's the way the Indians
    because they do that by their power.
So that shows the Indian,
    they had a power those days.
But now I don't think so.
Nobody can do that.

Prophecy at Lytton

A long time ago (maybe as long as two thousand years ago) a large group of people lived at the junction of the Fraser and Thompson rivers, where Lytton is today. Among them was a boy and his grandmother. The boy was lazy. The people blamed his grandmother for his bad habits. They felt that she had not trained him properly. When they could stand his laziness no longer, the people abandoned them both to starve, or so they thought.

At one time in Lytton, there was a lot of Indians
  right at Lytton where the town is now.
Up on the hillside, from there to the east like,
  in the hillside.
That's where the Indians lived at that time.

That's a long time ago.
  I would say that was before Christ.
That was right after the animal-people,
  shortly after the animal-people,
    when it's become to be real people, Indian.

And those days, there is no Christ yet.

And God came to certain one to talk to 'em.
Not for all of 'em, but certain one.

But, when he going to draw the animal-people from the animal,
  God came at that time,
    and he see all the people at that time.
That was long time before this happens in Lytton.
That's another way.

But this in Lytton,
  God came all right at that time.

168

There was a lot of people, Indian, live there
   and they got a teepee there and there and there.
A lot of teepees, you know.
Bunch of Indian.

And those days, the Indian,
   all they do is hunting and fishing.
And they got the berries, you know, pick the berries,
   and get the digging, you know, the root digging.
That's food too.
And the berries, and the deer, and the fish,
   that's all they do.
They just getting the food.
They busy everyday.
They go out hunting,
   and some people they do something else.
And they were living in one area, like a lot of people.

And the one old lady, not too old,
   could be around sixty years old, something like that.
And she got a daughter, and she got a son-in-law,
   and these two, they both die,
      not at the same time,
         but I think one of them died first.
And not too long and the other one died.

And these two, they had a son.
And they both died, you know.
But this old lady, she take care of the son of her daughter.
And that was her grandson.
See?
She take care of 'em.

And this little boy,
   he could be around one year old or two when his mother died.
Then his dad died.
But he's living with his grandmother.

And all the people, they hunt, and they getting food.
And whoever is old and they can't hunt,
   and they can't do much work,

they give 'em from their food what they get to live.
But they can do a little work at the camp, you know.
Might gather in some wood or something else.
Just what they can do.

And at this time this old lady, she raise that boy.
From one or two years old,
   she raise him up to eight or ten years old.
But she don't train him.
She never tell him,
   "Do this work.
     Go with these people to get the meat.
     Pack 'em in."
She just leave 'em alone.

And the boy was never told what to do.
Never was trained to be good worker,
   to be a good boy.

He just grow up like wild grass or something.
And he don't know nothing.
And he was lazy.
But he know enough to eat.
And he can eat like a pig.
He eat lots.

But the other people know how much work they do
   to get the food.
They got to work.
They all know.

But this boy, he don't know that,
   because was never told about it by his grandmother.
Maybe the other people told 'em, but he wouldn't listen.
Unless his grandmother could tell 'em something,
   he might take her word.
But in another way, he don't care.
And that means he's a bad boy.

Some people, they get a deer.
The next morning, mayber three or four of them,

they go over there and get the meat.
Those days, no horses, no nothing.
Only pack 'em on their back.

He should go.
His grandmother should tell 'em,
   "You go with these people and help them pack the stuff in."

But he never.

And these people go to get the meat, pack 'em in.
And the boy, he played around.
He don't pay no attention to what his people do.

But he eat as well as these others.

And these other people, they don't like that way.
And they told the old lady,
   "Why don't you make that boy work?
    And why don't you tell him to do something?"

Well, the old lady, she wouldn't tell him.
And she always give him food, you know, to live.

And one day, the bunch of Indians,
   they decided they're going to leave this boy and his grandmother
      because it was his grandmother,
         it was her fault for that boy to be like that.
That's why they're going to leave 'em,
   the both of 'em, and they can go away.

And they can stay there just themselves.
See what they can do.
They can be starve to death.

So all the people, they decided they'll do that.
And they talk to one another without the old lady know.

And one day, the people, they told the boys,
   like the same age as that bad boy,
      told these boys,

"You take that boy out, away, way out some place.
   Play and go away.
   And tell him some kind of thing to go out of sight.
   When he go out of sight, you guys come back,
      and when you get here, we all go away.
   When he come back, there'll be nobody here.
   But he wouldn't know which way the people went."

And they tell the ladies the same way for his grandmother.
And they go out, and they digging some roots or picking berries,
   and they tell this lady,
      "There's a lot of berries over there," or something,
      "You go over there and see 'em."

So, she go over there by herself.
Alone.
And she went out of sight.
And these other ladies come back,
   and they all go to the camp,
      and they gather the stuff, not much, you know.
Just get something and pack and go away.

And they hide their tracks.
They went in the place where the tracks couldn't be seen.

And the boy, he was out there and come back.
And the other boys, they're not there.
He missing the other boys.

The same way the old lady.
She come back and the other ladies, they're not there.
So finally the old lady get back to the camp first.
Nobody.
Everybody go.
She don't know which way it went.

And the boy came back.
Nobody at the camp.
Only his grandmother.

And they ask one another,

"Why? Where's the other ones?"

They don't know.

And they figure they're going to look around
  and see if they could see the tracks, which way they went.
And they looked around.
They couldn't see no track because these people,
  they hide their tracks.
They pick out hard ground so the tracks wouldn't show.
They couldn't find the tracks
  and they don't know which way their people went.

They go away.
They know where they were left.
They know these people left them.
So nothing they could do but stay there.

And when the people were there, before they leave,
  and they eat the meat, the bone of the deer,
    they put 'em away from the camp.
And they're there.
And they go over there and pick them up
  and bring 'em and boil 'em.
And all they can do is drink the soup of that bone.
But that's not good, you know.
They can't live on that kind of food.

Then, the old lady is kinda old.
She can go out and pick berries and dig — root digging.
But she can't do much because she's old.
And the boy is too young.
And, in another way, he don't know nothing.
He can never bring the food in.

So the way it look like,
  they going to stay there till they die by starving.
No eat nothing.

And these people, the other people, they go away.
Make another camp over there.

And then they hunt and they getting the food.
   "To heck with the boy and his grandmother!
      Let 'em starve to death!"

Because they blame the old lady.
That was the old lady's fault.
That's why the boy was no good.
If she train that boy, when that boy grow up,
   he'll be a good boy like the others.
And that'll be all right.
But she didn't.
That's why they leave 'em.

But they all mad,
   like they all mad to that lady and that boy, these Indian.

But God did not mad for these two.
Didn't.

So, they were live there for quite a while
   and they try to do what they can.
But still, it was all right in the summer.
But when winter comes, what they going to do?
They going to die by starving.

And the old lady, she make a bow and arrow.
Small.
And she give 'em to the boy.
And she said to the boy,
   "You go out.
      If you see a squirrel or magpie or bluejay or robin,
         whatever it is, the bird and the squirrel, or rabbit,
            if you see them,
               you shoot 'em with a bow and arrow.
      And bring 'em in. We can eat 'em."

All right.
Now she try to train that boy.
But it seems to be kinda late before they try train 'em.

So anyway, the boy, he go out and he look around.

And he see the magpie.
Shoot 'em with the bow and arrow and he got 'em.
And bring 'em.
When he get them in, he skinned 'em, you know.
He pull the skin and he skinned 'em.
And stretch out the skin while they're raw.
Just like the skin you throw over there.
And stretch 'em out and leave 'em dry.
He want 'em to be dry.
That would be bluejay skin.

Then next time, he mighta get a magpie.
Yeah, he get a magpie and he do the same.
He bring 'em in and skin 'em.
Then they eat the meat.
They boil 'em and eat 'em.
But they skin 'em and stretch out the skin.
Little pieces.
Magpie skin and bluejay skin.

And they do that until they had a few of that skin.
And they put it in.
They sewed it together.
Like, they put the bluejay skin, like, put it in here.
Magpie skin in here.
And bluejay skin, like, from one to another.
They mix 'em, this bluejay, magpie, and bluejay and magpie again.
Just like that all the way.
Then, they had 'em pretty good size.
It's all mixed, but it's all spotted because the magpie,
   it's black and white, and the bluejay, just blue.
But they had the bluejay in one section, and magpie here,
   and magpie here again, and bluejay here again.
It look nice, you know.

They stretch 'em out when they dry and sewed 'em up together,
   and then stretch 'em out.
They no good for nothing,
   because it's easy to tore.

But they laid 'em on the ground.

But only thing is, they just look nice.
That's all.

So, they have that.

And nothing more he can do but getting magpie and bluejay,
   and sometimes he get rabbit.
Or sometimes he mighta get squirrel.
But he never take the skin off that to use for anything.
Just skin 'em and eat 'em.

They live there quite awhile in the summer.
Then, they getting hungry.
They got quite a time to live, you know.
They could hardly eat, because they can't get 'em.
Sometimes the boy, he couldn't get no bluejay
   or magpie or rabbit or squirrel.
He can't get 'em.
But sometimes he get 'em.

And the old lady tried to get the root digging.
But she's old.
She can't do much work.

Then, they couldn't get no fish from the river,
   because they can't do it — and for quite a while.
And they begin to drop, you know.
They going to be weak because no eat.
Nothing to eat.
They eat very little.
That won't do 'em good, you know.
They drop down.
Pretty soon they'll be die by starving.

And this time, the boy went out and got the bluejay and magpie,
   two of them.
And that's a big one, a big food, one bluejay and one magpie.
They bring 'em in both, and skin 'em and boil the meat.

And they got them cooked.

They were ready to eat.
They got 'em cooked,
  and they make kind of a table
    and put the branches on the ground.
Then they put the meat there.
And then they sitting down there.

They were just ready to eat and somebody came.
They never see where he come from.
Just like if we could see somebody come,
  we'd say,
    "Here comes somebody."
But this one here, they never see.

The first thing they know,
  somebody stand right here.
Look like it was a man, old man.
And this old man, he says,
  "Looks like I come in time.
    You guys going to have lunch."

Old lady says,
  "Yeah, we're just going to have lunch."

The old lady says,
  "All right, you sit down and we'll all eat
    because you're in time.
    We just going to eat when you come.
    Sit down and we'll all eat."

But that's all the food they got.
Just a bluejay and magpie, that's all.
But still they offer this to their visitor.
They offered something from there.

All right, they all sit down,
  and this man told 'em,
    "I'm going to tell you something before we eat."

All right.
This old man told 'em,

"You close your eyes and you close your eyes.
  Two of you, close your eyes.
  I'm going to say a prayer."

Well, at that time, they don't say a prayer.
But anyway, they meant that way.
And told 'em,
  "I can do the talking, just a few words.
  Then I stop.
  And then I tell you,
    'All right, you can open up your eyes.'
  And you open up your eyes, and then we eat."

All right.
They close their eyes.
Then listen to him.
And he talk a few words.
And he said,
  "All right, open your eyes."

They opened their eyes.
Instead of magpie and bluejay there to eat,
  but they not there when they open their eyes.
They were different food there were there.
They never see that kind of food before.

And this old man told 'em,
  "We eat this one. There's lots of them there."

They never asked that man,
  "Where is that magpie and bluejay?"
They never said nothing about it.

Anyway, they started to eat this new kind of food.
And they eat.
And this man told 'em,
  "Eat all you want."

And the old lady, she think,
  This is not much.
But this man told 'em,

"Don't have to think that way.
 Eat plenty. You can eat all you want.
 We can eat all we want of this food.
 But still it'll be there.
 We never eat 'em all."

All right.
They eat till they get full.
And they had enough.
But the food is still the same.
There's never any less or any more.
Just about the same amount.

All right.
And this man told 'em,
  "This food that's there,"
    and suppose to be kind of cloth or something
      where the food was,
        and this man told 'em,
  "Put the cloth like that from this side.
   And put it away.
   You eat that again.
   But you got to say your prayer."
And told 'em what word they got to say in their language,
  because he's talking to them in their language.

Then he said,
  "You got to say your prayers.
   You got to say these words first.
   You put this food while it's cold like that.
   Put 'em away and bring 'em like that.
   The food's in there.
   Then you put 'em away.
   When you feel like eating, you hungry,
     bring 'em and put it here.
   Before you open 'em up, say your prayers.
   Say these word.
   And close your eyes and say that word
     just like I say awhile ago.
   Say that word.
   Close your eyes and say that word.

179

And after open 'em up and the food is there.
And eat that.
But not for all time.
That's just for so long.
Then there'll be no more.
But they will find there was something else
    when this food was no more, when they're gone.
You're not going to eat 'em all.
They'll be still the same.
But next time you open 'em, they'll be not there.
And then you'll know what to do after that."

All right.
They eat that.
And after they eat this food, and,
    they didn't know that was God yet.
Anyway, they just think he was just another man.
So he told 'em,
    he told the old lady,
        "This boy, did he get the bluejay and the magpie?"
        "Yeah, he get 'em.
        He shoot 'em with a bow and arrow.
        Sometimes he get a squirrel
            and sometimes he get a rabbit.
        That's about all he can get."

And he said,
    "Has he got a bow and arrow?"
    "Yeah."
    "Let me see it," man says.
And he showed it to him.
Only small.

And he told the old lady,
    "You know how to make this bow and arrow?"
    "Yeah, I know how to make 'em."

He says to the old lady,
    "You make a bigger one for the boy.
    This is only good for the bird, for the magpie, squirrel,
        and things like that.

Too small.
But you can make a bigger one,
   and strong and long arrow, strong,
      so he could shoot the deer with that and kill it.
   You make that bow and arrow and finish it
   and the boy could take that and go out."

And he told the boy,
   "When your grandmother finish that bow and arrow for you,
      when she finish 'em,
         then you can take that bow and arrow, big one,
            and you go out this way
               and you go out a little ways, not too far,
                  then you can see a deer just standing.
   You shoot it with the bow and arrow and you hit it,
      and you kill it.
   Then you come back and tell your grandmother.
   You both can go over there and cut 'em and skin 'em,
      and cut 'em into pieces and pack 'em.
    Pack 'em into the camp and dry 'em.
   Next two or three days, then you go out this way,
      and you go a little ways and you see a deer.
   And you kill 'em.
   Two, three days after that and you go out another direction.
   Everytime, until you make a round like.
   And don't you ever think,
      Well, this is lots of 'em. We got enough.
   Get all you can get.
   Then you can go down.
   You can make a net.
   You can make a net out of the grass they make a rope out of."

Tell the old lady,
   "You can make a net and you go down to the river.
    And you wait there awhile
      where is good for the salmon to come up.
    And you wait there a little while.
    Not too long.
    You could see salmon coming and you get 'em with that net.
    And you can get five or six, or maybe only two.
    And keep them.

And if there's a lot of them,
   cut 'em into pieces.
Dry 'em.
Do that all the time.
And this food will be no more because you're getting some.
Getting some meat and fish, root digging, and berries,
   and things like that.
And then you have a lot of food.
But don't you think this is enough.
Get all you can.
Because these people that were here,
   these people that leave you guys,
     over there where they are, they hungry.
They never get anything.
They couldn't get 'em.
Once in awhile maybe they get one deer.
They run out of food and they getting hungry.
And they going to have a heck of a time.
One of these days, they going to come.
Not all of them, but maybe one or two from there.
They're going to co:
And when you have lots of meat already dry,
   and a lot of fish already dry,
     and when you have a lot of them,
       you put them in a place where they keep the food."

And tell 'em in each place where they move,
  their teepee, the place,
   they still there where they put the food, you know.

And tell 'em,
  "Whenever you got lot of this dry meat,
   put them in that place.
  That's for that people.
  And in the other one, that's for that people.
  So many of them.
  You can put all the meat you dried,
   and you eat some of that.
  But put it there.
  That's for them when they come back.
  And, before they come back,

maybe only one or two they could come
   to see if you guys were alive yet.
And they don't have to come right here,
  but they might come on the distance
   so you could see them from quite a ways.
Then they go back.
Whenever you see them, the first time just see them,
  pay no attention, like you didn't see 'em.
But the second time, they could come,
  maybe three or four.
Same way.
They can pick out from the distance.
And you'll be around.
The first time they pick out from the distance,
  just like you didn't see 'em.
Pay no attention.
And they go back.
When they get back to their bunch,
  and they could tell their bunch,
    'These two, they was still there.
    They were alive.'
They were around in that same place.
That's what they'll have to say when they get around
  to the other ones.
But later on in a few days,
  they'll send three or four of them.
And they come the same way, like,
  pick out,
    then you could see there was four of them.
All right.
This time you wave your hand and tell 'em to come.
Tell 'em to come by your hand, you know.
Tell 'em to come.
Wouldn't be long and they'll sneak to you guys,
  and they'll get here.
And as soon as they get here they could look and say,
  'By God, there's a lot of meat over here.'
Then over there, then over there.
Then where you are there's all kinds of meat,
  all kinds of food.
They could look at it.

183

First they could be wonder how you could get 'em.
And you could tell 'em,
  'All right, you guys, sit down and I'll give you
    something to eat.'
And they'll be glad because they're hungry.
And then you give them some of this meat or fish or berries.
Anything you got, give 'em all they can eat.
And let them eat all they want till they get full.
Then you make a bundle.
Big one.
And tell the other one,
  'You pack this.'
And make another one, and say,
  'You pack this.'
All of 'em.
You make four bundles.
And tell 'em.
  'When you get back to wherever you was,
    and open this and you people can eat.
   Feed the people over there.'
And this one, they'll take it over there.
Just for that time.
Tell these people, these four, tell 'em,
  'When you get back and eat these,
    in two or three days, come back,
     all of you come back.
   Here's your camp.
   There's a lot of food there.
   And here's your camp.
   A lot of food there.
   And there, and there.
   And the food, it's all ready for you guys.
   Come back and stay here like it was before.'
 You tell 'em that."

All right.
That's what this man told 'em.

And after he told 'em all about this, he says,
  "What's this?"

That was the bluejay and magpie.
It was laid on the ground.
It look nice.

   "And what's this?"

   "That's the bluejay and magpie.
   We sewed 'em together.
   It's no good for nothing.
   Only lay on the ground.
   It look nice.
   That's all.
   Just look pretty."

This man says,
   "All right.
   Could you guys give me this?
   I want 'em."
   "Sure, you can take it. We give it to you."
And the man says,
   "All right. I'll take it."
And he reached down and picked 'em up.
And he held 'em in his hand.

And he says to this grandmother and grandson,
   he said to them,
      "You guys give me these. Now it's mine.
      But I'm not going to take it along with me.
      But still it's mine.
      I'm going to set 'em back on the same place.
      Then it's going to be there for all time.
      But it's going to turn in different way."

   "All right.
   You can do as you like.
   We give it to you."

   "Now this is the time," he told them.
   "I am the God.
   I'm the Father.
   I come from Heaven.

And your people left you.
They want you to be starved to death.
But I don't like it that way.
I don't want you people to starve to death,
   and also this bunch.
I want you to live.
But only thing is, these people got to come back and live
   just like it was before.
But I'm going to leave.
You're going to watch me.
I'm going back to the Heaven.
And this place, this country, this world
   not this world, but where you were here,
      all this place, it's yours.
And you going to live there till you die.
But whoever is next is going to be here at all time.
This is yours.
But another thing I'm going to tell you.
There was some people going to come here,
   not right away, maybe a long time from now.
They going to come.
I want 'em to come.
Different people.
Built just like you, only taller.
These people they going to get here is white.
More white than you.
You kinda dark.
But the people, they going to come here, is going to be whiter,
   whiter than you.
Long time from now they going to come here.
When they get here, that's going to be your,
   you're going to be amongst with them.
They going to live here.
When they come here, they going to live here for all time.
And you people going to be live together around here.
But these white people, when they come,
   they going to do the work.
They can make the land to be look good,
   just like this bluejay and magpie.
You guys make 'em look nice.
Very nice.

So the white people,
   they going to make this land very nice.
But still, you going to be there.
And whatever they going to make,
   just like I do now,
      give you the food for you to live,
         they can do the same.
When they get here, they can go to work
   and they can change everything,
      what you eating.
And they'll give you from what they do or what they raise,
   because this is your place.
But they going to do the work.
And what they get, they can give you some of that.
And they could use themselves."

That means the white people is going to come.
And that's the way it's going to be.
And that's the way they do now.
The white people came and they fixed the land,
  make a hayfield, and make a garden.
They do everything nice.
But when the Indian only here, they don't make it that way.
Nothing.
All they do, just hunt.

And told 'em,
  "When these people come here,
      they going to be amongst you people.
   They going to live here with you.
   But this is your place."

And he said,
  "When you go out to get that deer, it's all yours.
   It's going to be that way for a long time."

And he don't tell 'em,
  "Later on you going to have a permit to get that deer."
He never say that.
But now, the Indians, they going to hunt.
And they have to go to the government office

187

and ask for the permit.
And the government office, they write.
It say, "Here is your permit to hunt."

It should not be that way.
The Indians should be free.
They can go out hunt.
But the white people, that's their way.

They can go to the office and get the permit for what they can shoot,
   buck or doe, or one or three or four, or only one.
That's for the white people, not for the Indians.
Because, at that time, God, he never said for the Indian,
   "Later on you going to have a permit to get the deer."
He never did say that.

As long as he don't say that, well,
   Indians supposed to be free at all times that way.
Not only that way.
For everything.

So he tell 'em all about and they said,
   "These people, when they get here, long time from now," he says,
   "I want 'em to come here.
    But not all.
    The part of it, it's going to be here, but the other part of it
      going to be still over there where they are now."

Well, that means in Europe.
See? The white people came.
But still there's lots more over there.
And now there is over there in England,
   a lot of white people, all over in Europe.
But there's lot of 'em in here.
But that time, when God was there at Lytton,
   there is not a white man in this place.
Only Indian.

And that's the reason why the Indian, they was saying,
   "This is my land."
They don't say,

"This world is mine."
Because the world,
  it belong to all person, whoever they were,
    living alive in the world.
You, me, or anybody.
But, in another way, the Indians owns this island.
Not on overseas.
This one, this island, supposed to be for the Indian.
They are living here in the first place.

And that's another stories.
They become to live here in the first place
  long before the white man came.
In the first place was animal-people.
That's when they was "imbellable"* stories.
But then, in Lytton, they were already in human people
  when God came and told 'em,
    "Now, tell you all this and you got to remember.
    You will see these people.
    That's going to be your friend.
    When they live here, they going to be your friend.
    Not to fight one another. Not to make trouble.
    Going to be your friend.
    But they going to live here
      from this time till the end of the world."

And who knows when it's going to be the end of the world?
But he told 'em they going to live here till the end of the world.
And you too.
But now, nobody here but only you Indian.
He said,
  "Now I leave.
  And you going to see me going up.
  I come from Heaven.
  I am the Father. I am God."
He said,
  "This one here, you give me, that's the bluejay skin and magpie.

---

*This is the English translation Harry was given for *chap-TEEK-whl*, stories from "way back" during "the time of the animal-people." Once, when seeking an English translation for *chap-TEEK-whl*, Harry was told these stories are "unbelievable." Since that time, Harry has called them "imbellable" stories.

        They look nice.
        I'm going to put them down and stand."
Because when they sewed 'em, you know,
    then it's a pretty good size.
And he said,
    "I'm going to put them down because it's mine.
    You give it to me.
    And I'm going to put 'em down.
    And I'm going to stand right on 'em.
    And then I'll go."

All right.
He put that down.
Then he walked over there and stand right on 'em.
Supposed to be a skin, a bird skin, you know.
But they never tore.
He put 'em down and stand there.
It's big, you know.
They sewed 'em together and then they was so big.

Stand there, and then he said,
    "All right.
    Just watch me.
    I'm going back."

Then he was stand on that bluejay skin.
And he stand,
    and they just like,
        jerk!
Down.
Up he goes.

And he don't go fast.
He go kinda slow.
Not too fast.
Not fly up, you know.
You know, he go kinda slow.
And they watch 'em.
Way up.
And they could still see 'em.
Like a smoke.

Just like a smoke, and they don't see 'em no more.
And they look.
No more.
Went up to the sky.
And then they look at the one they,
   that skin they stand on.
They looked there.
Turn into a rock.
It's a rock.
Turn into a rock, just like this one here.*
Used to be wood at one time, but it turn into a rock.

That's how come.
From that time it can happen that way.
Then it was.
And that's supposed to be wood but they turn into a rock.
Because that bluejay skin and magpie,
   it was a skin, but God stand on 'em
      and raise from there.
And instead, they watch him going up, you know.
It takes awhile.
Watch 'em till he go away.

And then looked there.
As soon as they looked there, it's already rock, just like this.
But still, the spot, it's still there.
Still look nice.
But it turn into a rock.
And it's heavy.
It's thick and big.

And that, in Lytton, from the town is now,
   up to the hillside, that way,
      that's where that is.
And this rock is there.
For a long long time, all the Indians, they was seeing 'em,
   they still in the same place.

---

*Harry points to a fossil which he had found and saved for many years.

191

And he told 'em,
   "This one here, I'm going to stand on.
   I'm going to raise from there.
   But this one, leave 'em as they are.
   Leave 'em there all the time.
   Don't take 'em away.
   Just leave 'em there."

So, it was there a long time till the white people come.
One at a time, maybe a few this way and a few that way.
Just a very few white people came.

And this one is still there.
But the white people didn't know.
They never seen 'em.

And later on, the white people,
   getting thicker and thicker and thicker.

And finally, the oldtimer, like, way back,
   could be around 1850, could be maybe before then,
      maybe 1800, something like that,
         because old John Ashnola, John Shiweelkin
            born in 1820.
And on his time, it's already disappeared, that rock,
   when he know.
When this rock disappeared, it might be before 1800,
   something like that.
But the white people, you know, they already came.

And the Indians at that time, they say,
   they decided and they say,
     "We better hide that rock.
     We going to sunk 'em in the ground.
     Because the white people came, and they might find 'em.
     It's not very big.
     It's just so big, and thick.
     It's heavy.
     But still, the white people,
       they might find 'em and take 'em away.
     They'll pack 'em away.

They could steal that from us.
But we could sunk 'em down right there and bury 'em.
So the white people will never see that."

All right.
That's what they figure,
  the Indians at that time.

So, they went over there
  and then they dig just along side of 'em.
Like, they lay on the hillside.
There is a little dip, like,
  not steep, but it's uphill a little bit.
And they dig on the lower side.
They dig it deep enough
  and just slide 'em and drop 'em in the hole.
And bury 'em and smooth this.
But they got some kind of mark,
  not there, but a long ways off from there.
But they know how many steps from there to that mark.

Just like they do when surveying.
I work on surveying and we do that.
We put in a stick or nail, the bar, like just about this size,
  and we drive 'em.
Sticking out just a little bit.
And they got to stand on top, you know.
Then they put the line from that to the tree,
  maybe long ways out.
Then they mark that,
    how many feet from that tree to which way,
      which direction, either west or south or north or whatever it is,
        or angle, you know,
          how many degrees to the west or to the south, from that mark.
Then the post was there.
And the next surveyor, in seventy or eighty years,
  they could still find that.
Easy to find.

Same thing they do.
They put in the ground

and they had some kind of mark, way out,
    not one, but maybe two or three.
And they know how far from there to there.
And they know where it's supposed to be,
    in open place, when they bury 'em.

But they never tell the young people, the young Indian.
They tell some.
But later on, they just quit telling 'em.
And they don't tell 'em anymore.

And now today,
    all the young people in Lytton and Spence's Bridge and Shulus,
        and everywhere,
            they don't know that.
They never did know it was buried there.
They don't know anything about it today.

That's the way they want,
    the Indian was.
Supposing they figure,
    if they let the young people know,
        and nowadays, that they could tell the white people,
            and they could sell it.
They going to get the money from the white people for that rock.
They might ask $500 or something like that.
And the white people will give 'em that money.

And whoever they sell that,
    maybe a bunch or something like that,
        and then take the money.
Have a lot of money to drink.
It can be that way, they figure.
So they don't let 'em know.

And not yet.
They never did let 'em know.
The way I see, nobody know today about that.

But I know.
And my wife know.

Because I learned that from her father.
And I learn the same story from my grandmother.
And so she learned that from her father.
And also we learned that from Mary Narcisse.
Mary Narcisse was living until 1944 until the age of 116.
That's how we know that.

But we didn't know if anybody know about that.
We think not, because nobody talked about it.
Not even Slim.
I never tell.
But one time I says to my wife,
   "We both know about that spotted rock in Lytton, you and I."
   "Yeah," she says, "I know."
I said,
   "Next time we go to Josephine George,"
      that's the Indian doctor,
        "next time we go over there,
           you ask Josephine about that.
    See what she got to say."
We bring some fruit.
We want her to work on us because she's a doctor.
We were there two or three days.
And my wife and Josephine,
  they go to bed together in one bed.
And my wife ask her all about it.
My wife tell her the stories.
Not all.
Just a part of it.
Just a little.
Says,
   "There's supposed to be a spotted rock over in Lytton.
   It was there.
   What happened to it?"
But we know, but she ask Josephine,
  "What happened?
  Did you ever know about it?"
And Josephine, she don't like to say.
She know, but she hide it.
But she's the only one left.
And maybe Antony Joe,

another old one still alive.
Just a few of those old people know about it
  but they never said a word.
And Josephine don't like to say anything.
But my wife explain that she know that we did know,
  just like she does.
So finally she says to my wife,
  "I'm kinda surprise that you two, you and your husband,
    know about this.
   We thought nobody know but just a few of us around here.
   But how do you know?"
My wife told her,
  "We learn that from my father, and from my husband's grandmother
    and that Mary Narcisse."
She mention all these people.
That's how we learn — from these old people.
Because they go over there to get some salmon
  kinda often in the early days.
From here they go to Spence's Bridge, Lytton, Hope, Lillooet,
  on horseback those days.
And these old people, when they were over there,
  they learn that.
Then when they come back, we learn from them.
So my wife told Josephine all about that.
Then she could tell that we did know.
Then she says,
  "They hide that."
She says,
  "We know that already. We know they hide it."
But we just wondering what we got to say.
I could ask 'em myself, but I can't ask her in her language.
But my wife can speak in her language.
And she ask her.
And for a while she don't like to say,
  but she can tell that we did know.
So she tell all about it.
She said,
  "We don't want to tell the young people nowadays
    because they're going to sell 'em.
   I never tell nobody since.
   You're the first one because you ask for it.

And I try to tell some Indians about it.
They don't care.
They don't seem to want to know."

So that's all.

PART THREE:
STORIES OF POWER

Harry and Matilda at their huckleberry-picking camp in the Tulameen Valley, 1948.

A Boy Receives Power
From Two Birds

A boy is travelling along a trail, when all of a sudden he hears someone singing. He sees no one, however, except two birds sitting in a nest.

That's the way they get their power.

You can see this?
This is a bench,
  on the bench, you know, not high.
Bench is not high.
But there was a trail that go down there
  from the top of the bench to the bottom.

And this boy
  when he was a boy,
    that could be somewhere around eleven years old, maybe ten,
      something like that.
And he was going along,
  like, from here.
And he figure he going to go
  and he can go down to that little trail
    and he know that was a little trail.

So he was travelling from here to there.
And when he come to the bench,
  the edge of the bench, like,
    and he could hear someone was singing a song,
      but he couldn't tell where.
He could just hear.
Sound like to the bottom of the bench,
  or in the air someplace, maybe on the tree.
There was some big trees on the bottom, like.

Anyway, he thought maybe he better go here
    and right to the edge of that bank.
There was a trail that way.
Then he could see from there down.
Not very high.
Just a low bench.
And he might hear who was singing,
    who was singing the song.

And he walk some more,
    and he come right to the edge of the bench,
        and he look down.
See nothing.
Anyway, he thought maybe get down
    at the bottom,
        and he could see this maple bush was standing
            just alongside the trail
                and close to the hill at the foothill.

So he think he can get down there.
He might see 'em because he want to see 'em.
So he walk down on that trail
    and he get to the foothills, that's right here,
        and the maple bush alongside him,
            and close to the trail,
                and close to the hillside.
And sounds like it was singing on this bush,
    big bush, maple bush, you know.
Big one.
Get down, stop there,
    and he look up at the bush.
Then he could see the bird nest
    just small
        while he were at the bottom.
Looked that way through the bush
    and he could see that.
Watch 'em a little while.
Sounds like they're singing there.

But he don't see.
He see the nest.

But the first thing he know, the one bird,
  it fly out of that nest
    and it fly from that bush.
It fly and past him.
And it fly that way for a ways
  and then it looked that way and watch him.

Go a little ways on the air.
It fly not too high and it turned around and come back.
And come back while he was watching that way.
Seen 'em fly that way.
Then he could still hear another one was singing a song
  up in that bush.

Then the first thing he know
  the bird, it fly back while he was standing there.
First thing he know somebody standing alongside him
  was a young lady.
Looked at him,
It was a young lady, standing there.
But it was a bird in the first place
  when he seen 'em fly.

Just like one second he seen 'em standing there
  and she was a young lady.
And told him,
  "Well boy, you're here."
  "Yeah."
And told him,
  "You just happen to run in with us.
   We have little trouble.
   This is my sister up there."

And he take a look.
He seen that nest before when they get down
  and he take a look.
And that was the same nest, but they big.
Great big nest.
And he see another lady was sitting in there
  just about here.
He couldn't see this way because nest is kinda deep.

He could see this way.

And this other one told 'em,
  "You see that's my sister.
   She have a little trouble.
   She was going to have a birth
     but she got trouble, and she call me.
   I live quite a ways down.
   She call me and I come to help."

That's all she tell him.

And this other one up there,
  she could be about this way up there.
Then she talk, and told him,
  "Yeah, I did call my sister.
   She don't live around here.
   This way, quite a ways
     and there was a lake and the lake was long.
   In the other end of the lake was beautiful bushy land.
   That's where my sister lives,
     but I been in trouble and I call her.
   In a little while she get here and help me.
   And now we getting over.
   You just run into us just in time.
   Just when you come to the edge of that bank,
     we getting to be okay.
   And, I'm going to tell you now.
   From now on
       you don't have to do that when you're young,
         but that's going to be your job.
   You're going to be a doctor that way.
   After you get to middle age or more,
       we will let you know
         when its time for you to do the work.
   We'll let you know.
   Then this song,
     we'll sing this song.
   Then you could learn.
   Then keep that in your mind.
   Long time.

We'll let you know when it's time for you to work.
And you could sing that song.
Then think of us.
Now we get together here, the three of us."

And then they tell him what he should do
  and so on, you know.
Then she started to sing,
  that one that's in the nest there.
And the other one sing.
And he sing too.
They all sing together,
  him, and the other lady in the ground standing there.
But the other one, she's up on the nest.
They sing this song for a while.
Then told him,
  "All right, that'll do.
   Sometime, long time, we'll let you know
     whenever we think it's time for you to do the work.
   You not going to do this work often,
    but maybe once in awhile.
   Later on when some people,
     sometime, maybe they're going to have a birth,
      they might get trouble.
   If they do, the others go get you.
   You can mention this when you sing
    in the wintertime dance,
     in the wintertime like they do the powwow.
   You're going to do that later on
    when you get to middle age.
   You could sing that song in two winters.
   At the second winter, you sing that song.
   When you finish, you tell the people
    that you're going to do that kind of a work.
   You tell 'em what you supposed to do so they'll know.
   Whenever it happens
    the people know you're going to do it
     and they can go get you and bring you.
   Then you can do the work for the womens
    who's gonna have a baby but she has a hard time.
   Then you can do the work

205

and this is the way you're going to do it."

They tell him all about it.

"So all right, now we're going to part."

So the first thing he know,
    and he musta drop down.
Sleep.
It was in the daytime when he met them,
    but he was sleep for quite a while.

So he wake up.
That's where he was standing.
He musta go from there a little ways,
    then drop and sleep there for a long time.
They say it's not noon yet.
Could be eleven o'clock or half-past ten
    or maybe eleven o'clock,
        that is, if they got time,
            but they haven't.
It's not noon yet.
He don't know no more.
He went sleep
    but first thing he know
        the sun was way down.
Getting towards evening when he wake up.
And he don't see them no more.

And this bird,
    I don't know the name of that bird in English.*
In Indian name, *spoo-AL-kin.*
Their head was red, just like that over there,
The whole head was red,
    and more like a bluejay.
They got more hair on the top of their head.
But all red,
    but the rest was kinda mixed, mixed feather.

---

*The bird is known in English as the pileated woodpecker (*dryocopus pileatus*), a crow-sized woodpecker with a red crest.

206

Kinda black and white, and red,
   not quite red.
Kinda spotted, you know.
But on the head, just pure red.
The size about like the robin.
Then they always go to a tree
   and kinda make a hole on the bark, you know.
There's two kinds.
One of them was small.
Woodpecker, yeah, that's the little one.
But this other one that's supposed to sing,
   that *spoo-AL-kin*, that's a little different kind.
Nearly the same.
That woodpecker, I know that.
But this other one, it has a name,
   but it's a little different.

So that was the one he found,
   himself, he found.
He found it.
And this is the one told him what he should do
   when he get to be middle age.
And then he remember that,
   but he don't tell nobody
      till he comes to be about thirty years old,
         something like that.
Then he sleep and he see that in his dream.
See this bird again.
And she told him,
   this is winter, could be like in the fall,
      in October or November,
         "Now, this coming winter,
            when winter come,
               you going to put up a dance
                  and you can sing your song.
            Then let the people come and sing and dance.
            Do that twice.
         Next winter do that again.
            On the second winter, when you finish,
               you tell the people, whoever they were there,
                  you tell them what you going to be.

You going to be a doctor.
Tell them all about what you going to be
    so they'll know.
Whenever it happens, people will get you
    and bring you.
Then you can do the work."

He say that in the fall.
Then he tell his wife and he tell the other people,
  "I am going to sing this winter.
  Get everything ready.
  When winter come, I'm going to sing."

So he do that.
Next winter he do the same.

But on the second winter, when he finish singing,
  and he tell the people,
    "Now, the second winter I sing,
      and I'm going to tell you what I'm going to be
        from now on.
    I'm going to be a doctor, Indian doctor."

He is supposed to go and see whoever is sick, like me.
Anybody, woman or man or children, or anybody.
Any sickness.
When they sick, somebody, they can tell him.
And he can go over there and work on 'em.
And get him better.
And he said,
  "I can do that, but this is going to be a special job.
  I can do that too.
  When some woman, she's going to have a baby,
    if she got stuck, if she got trouble,
      that's going to be kinda special.
  But you can go get me.
  I can do the work on that too."

So, he's supposed to do in two different kinds of work.
All right.
After that, he was an Indian doctor.

If somebody was sick and the people say
    he's an Indian doctor,
        "Go get him
            and see what he can do with the one that's sick."

So they went and get him
    and he come and he work on the sick people,
        sick man or woman or children.
He get 'em better.
He do that kinda often, you know,
    every once in awhile.
He's a real Indian doctor.

But, once in awhile, those women those days, no hospital,
    not like now.
Sometimes, maybe some woman, she's going to have a baby,
    and the baby wouldn't born, she's got a hard time.
They all know that.
And they say to one another,
    "Go get him.
     He's supposed to do this."
So, whoever they are, they have to get saddle horse
    and they lead one horse with the saddle on,
        because he might have a horse,
            but he mighta be turned loose, hard to find.
It takes more time to find his horse.
He might as well take the horse that he's going to ride.

So they get there and bring him back right away.
So they lead the horse and they went for a ways,
    maybe ten miles, maybe fifteen miles,
        sometimes maybe from Penticton to over there,
            that takes longer.

And whoever they come tell him,
    "I come to get you.
     We have trouble over there."

And he know.
Just before somebody come to get him,
    and he know already in his power,

in his dream.
And he said to his people,
   "Somebody's coming to get me.
    There was some trouble that way."
He know that.
Then after awhile, maybe two or three hours after that
   and somebody come with a saddle horse and lead one horse.
And told him,
   "Come to get you."
   "All right."

And he ride the horse and away they go.
They go fast.
Go in the gallop.
Then they come to the place.
And those days they had a teepee.
That's their house — teepee.
And there was a fire inside.
And a few days before, and they built another one
   so this woman can have a birth in that teepee.
The old teepee, they always warm.
They have a fire there.
They always warm.
But they built another one.
Make fire in there so the other people can be in there.
But only the one, she going to have a birth,
   and the nurses, they can be in that old teepee.
They build another one, and then they might have a fire
   on the outside,
      so they can cook there and keep warm inside,
         but not in the old teepee.
Only the nurses, like, two or three women,
   maybe four, the older one, you know.

And, when he come, he get there and stop,
   stop the horses.
Then he get off.
If anybody, if they get off the horse,
   they had a stirrup, and they keep one foot on the stirrup,
      and keep the other foot, the right foot,
         first on the ground, getting off the horse.

When he get off, as soon as he touch the ground,
  just like, CLAP,
    something's taken from underneath his foot.
And right up.
And sing his song as loud, as fast as he can do.
Just as soon as he step on the ground.
And he sing the song loud.
Then turned around, and he can walk pretty slow.
Walk slow.
He step little at a time.
He make very little slow steps.
He get to the door.
Somebody could lift that curtain, you know,
  at the door, at the teepee.
But now there was a door like that.
And they can go in there.
Then, the old womens, that's supposed to look after the baby,
  when it come,
    and they could be over there in one side.
They might be laying in bed, on the ground,
  no bed like we have now.
And he walked that way slow
  about halfways from the door to the woman.
Then he stop.
And he sing the song.
And he put his hands to her like that, you know.
And he put it that way for a little while.
Then he said to these others,
  there's two, three, maybe four.
And he said,
  "Whoever is going to look after the baby when it come,
    they can go over there and they can be ready
      right there, good and ready.
  When they were ready there, then I can go.
  And when I get there,
    then I'm going to put my hand on top of her head.
  And one of them, they can go over there
    and be sitting there getting ready."

Then he walked slow, still sing his song
  and he walk slow till he get there.

211

And he put his hands like that,
   maybe two of them, you know,
      just like that.
And he said,
   "Now, watch."
And put the other hand on top of the woman's head
   because she lay, you know.
He put his hand, you know, like that,
   slow, and when he get to that,
      and kinda press it.
And he said,
   "I can press and I turn around fast and I go right out.
      Then you catch the baby."

So they do that.
Whoever they watch that, they're right there,
   and then he walk, just press it,
      then he turn around,
         and he walked fast and go out.
And before he do that, and he said,
   "I walk out fast.
      Then you get the baby right away.
      Then you fix him up. Wash him and do whatever you do.
      Do all what it has to be done,
         and finish everything,
            and one of you can go out.
      I'll be sitting by the fire there,
         in the other teepee.
      Then you could come and tell me,
         'Well, we got the new one.
          It come.
          Was a boy or girl.
          We already have 'em.'"
Then he said,
   "I can come back, sing my song,
      and come back.
   And I can straighten out this woman.
   Then I get my power from her,
         and that's all."

So he does that.

212

After he touch the woman's head and then press it down
  and then he turn right around fast and go right out.
Then he come to the fire
  and there were some people there,
    maybe some aunts, a lot of people there,
      and they sitting there and talk.
And these others, they have the baby,
  they talk.
They fix it up and they wash it
  and they do whatever they supposed to do.
And they finish.
And one woman go out and come to him and tell him,
  "Well, we have the new one."
Was a boy, or girl.

All right.
And he get up.
And he sing his song.
And the way he was, he walk kinda slow
  and go in and walk to her and stand there,
    and then he put his hand like that.
Fix it up for a little while,
  and then maybe a minute or two minutes, something like that,
    and then he said,
      "That's all right.
        I go home now."

Then he turn around, go out, and get the horse,
  and go home.
Everything is okay.

See?
He was told by that bird to do that.
And he was just a special man for that.
And in the others, any other kind of a sickness,
  he go to work.
They always get somebody better.
They don't lose but once in a while.
Because somebody's got to die anyway.
Sometimes they work on 'em but still they die.
Most of 'em, they get them better.

213

He's a real good doctor, that.
I seen him when he was very old.
He's about 85, maybe 90, maybe close to 100 when I seen him.
I know he was pretty old.
He lost one eye.
He got only one eye.
He don't do that work very often,
    maybe two, three times in his life.
I think the people say one time they took him to Penticton.
And another time just there, once or twice around there,
    because it don't happen that way too often,
        just once in awhile.
Those days if they didn't have any special doctors like him,
    when the woman get that way, then she die that way.
So, but when he, he can do work, you don't lose the one person.

So, that is the way he get his power — from the bird.
And this bird, she just happen to,
    must be eggs or something, you know.
And she just happen.
And the one that's going to have a birth,
    she got stuck and she just call her sister.
And nobody know how she call her,
    but she says,
        "Quite a ways, and there was a lake,
            and the other end of the lake,
                that's where my sister lives.
            And I call her. And she comes.
            And she gets here pretty fast.
            Get here right away."

She must have phoned her!
Well, the birds, the animals, they talk to one another
    just like on the phone.
Like from here, like, to maybe on top of the mountain,
    or way somewhere the other one.
This one here can talk to that.
Sometimes the coyote,
    maybe one of them, they bark on the hillside,
        in a little while, the other one bark over there.
Well, that means they were talking to one another.

We could hear 'em bark over there.
We could hear that, but we don't know what it means.
They're supposed to talk to one another.
All the animals, they do that,
   right from way back, right from "imbellable" stories
    and then it's that way from all time.
It's got to be a power person to get to understand them.
Not anyone.
It's got to be a power person.
That's the way it goes.
Those days, everybody [had power]
   but some, their power not strong as the others,
    but they got power, but not so strong.
But some of them, seems to be they got more power — better.
And that's why they have an Indian doctor.
And a lot of these people, some of them is not a doctor,
   not an Indian doctor, just a power person.
And their power, they can never use
   to see if they can get the sick people,
    get them better.
They can never do that,
   because they're not told by the other bird or animal,
    whatever they talk to 'em they have a power,
     they don't tell 'em to use your power for somebody else.
Just for himself, or if they got children.
They can use his own power for his own children,
   on his wife, and that's all.
Not for the others.
But the others was told by the bird,
   or animal, whatever they told 'em,
    they can do for anybody, they can use his power
     to anybody that was sick or get hurt,
      anything like that.
And that's what they call the Indian doctor.
But a lot of these, they got power,
   power man or power woman,
    but just only good for themselves or herself.
And is not told to use his power to somebody,
   but for him or for her.
That's the way it goes.
But the others was told,

so they call that an Indian doctor.
They got a right to do that work to anybody.
But the others didn't,
  so they wouldn't do, because he's not told.

A Woman Receives Power
From the Deer

A woman in Westbank is seriously ill. Two friends pay her a visit thinking that it will probably be their last. When they return just a few days later, they are shocked by what they find.

This LaLA
  she was a power woman,
    but she don't work for nobody.

And she got sick one time.
That's a few years ago.
Could be about twelve years ago.
Really sick.

And the people from Westbank,
  his name Eli.
Aleck Eli, him and his wife.
And they was going to go to Omak
  for the rodeo.
But they heard that old lady was pretty sick,
  that's their neighbour, you know.
They lived like from here to Charlie Allison,
  or maybe a little more.

And somebody told 'em the old lady was pretty sick.

Well, they gotta go and see the rodeo.
So, they thought,
  "We better go see the old lady.
    We go over and see 'em and then we go to Omak.
    She mighta be die.
    When we come back, she'll be dead.
    We better go and see 'em."

So they went over there and see 'em.
And she was pretty sick.
Watch 'em, looked at 'em for a little while.
I think he thought,
  "That old lady, maybe in a couple of days,
    she'll be no more."

Anyway, they went to Omak.
And when they're around in Omak, after the rodeo,
  two days over there, I think,
    and they come back,
      and when they get home,
        they ask somebody,
          "How's that old lady?"
          "Oh, all right.
            Still sick, but still all right."
          "We better go and see 'em again."

So they went.
Get to the house.
And she got a son.
Her son was out, out around the house, outside,
  working, you know,
    splitting wood or something, you know.
Get there and he says,
  "How's the old lady?"
  "Oh, she's all right."
And, they say,
  "We come to see 'em."
And this man tell 'em,
  "All right, you go in there and see 'em,
    but don't get surprise when you see 'em.
    It mighta be look different when you see 'em.
    You might be surprise."

So, they went inside and see her
  in the house, one room,
And they got a bed in there right on the floor.
And all the firs, you know,
  the branches,
    they broke them off from the tree.

218

That's the spruce branches.
And they put them on the floor.
And they put the light, the very light blanket, you know,
    put them on,
        and she lay there.
And other branches was kinda piled.
That was her pillow.
And the other branches, they broke 'em in big chunks, you know.
And they was laying on top of her, all branches.

Anybody would be kinda surprise,
    when they see that,
        a person lay that way,
            fir on top of 'em,
                lay on 'em, no blanket,
                    just lay on the branches.

Went over there and see 'em
    and, she says,
        "I'm getting all right. Getting better."

And later on, when she get better,
    when she get all right,
        she's quite a lady to talk.
Tell a lot of things.
And she says to Aleck and somebody else,
    and she says,
        "You seen me at that time,
            when you come and I was fixed up with the branches?"
        "Yeah."
    She says,
        "When I was a little girl, just small,
            as we were out in the hills hunting,
                my people were hunting and we got the camp
                    up in the mountain."
And she says,
    "One night my dad come back from hunting
        and there was a trail that way.
        I know that trail.
        I been go through that trail."

219

Says,
  "My dad coming along that trail,
    and come home and we eat supper
      and after supper it's getting dark."

And, she says,
  "My dad told me,
    'You go on this trail.
     You go to that creek.
     There was a little creek there.
     You know, the trail goes across the creek.'
     Says,
     'You can go to that creek.
      Before you get to the creek,
        on the side of the road,
          just a little ways from road,
            I left a deer right there.
       I killed a deer,
         and I drag him from the mountain,
           and I left him there.
       And I cut the heart off.
       And I put 'em inside the deer.' "

He clean 'em, you know, but he put the heart in again.

  "Says,
    'I was going to bring that heart,
      but I forget.
     You go over there
       and get 'em and bring the heart,
         because I want to eat that in the morning for breakfast.' "

Well, she's got to go.

So, she says she went on the trail
  in the dark quite a ways, maybe two miles.

Then, she says, she's going along the trail
  and she get near.
She knows where the creek is, you know.
And this side of the creek, on the side of the road,

before she get there,
   she get near,
      and she could hear somebody singing a song.
Over there.

And her dad told 'em,
   "If you heard something,
      if you see something,
         don't you run away.
      Don't you come back.
      Go over there."

She heard somebody singing not too far ahead of 'em.
And she's going that way.
She keep walking until she get close
   and she could see the deer was standing,
      standing right there.
And that was the one that sing.
That's a doe.

And she look at the other one was laying
   and she suppose to get the heart
      from that one that's laying there.
That was the dead one.
Her dad drag that deer from the mountain and left 'em there.

But there was another one standing there
   singing the song.
And the deer, the one that's standing,
   and told 'em,
      "Well, little girl, you come here and you met me.
      I was just going to leave when you come.
      I was just going to leave.
      This is my body, the one that lay there.
      That's my body.
      And this is another body.
      That's my body too, but it's another one.
      But this is my body.
      But this body, they leave that and I'm gone."

And told 'em what she could do

when she get older,
   when she get sick.
      "Look at that, my body."

Her dad, you know,
   when he left that deer there,
     and he broke some branches,
       then he put them on the ground,
         and they lay the deer on the branches,
         and he broke some more.
Then he put them over.
That's what they usually do, you know.

And the deer told 'em,
   "Look at that, my body,
     it was lay on the branches,
       then there's some branches over 'em.
    When you get sick, when you're really sick, you do that.
    You do the same,
       then you get all right."

That's just her.
They not supposed to do that to somebody.
Just for her.
That's for her own use.

She says,
   "That's the way I find out at that time.
    And now, since that time, that's the first time
     I use that and I get better."

So, that's a power woman,
   but just for herself.

A lot of these people like that in the old times.
Maybe today too.
Maybe she's a power man or a power woman,
   but she wouldn't work for nobody,
     just for herself.
But if she's got children,

well, she can use her power for her children
to get 'em save from getting hurt and things like that.

Two Men Receive Power
From Two Cranes

Two men go to the high mountains to hunt. At their camp, all is quiet save the trumpeting of a flock of cranes nearby. Later, in the evening as they sit by their fire, they are startled by the forms of two figures moving toward them, looking vaguely birdlike, vaguely human.

I'll tell you this.
That's not too long ago.
They got a horses those days,
    and they got a gun.
Not long ago.
Could be around a hundred years ago
    or maybe not that long.
And that was happened in the north, up this way.
So these two man, two Indians,
    someplace up in, I couldn't tell where,
        but up north anyway.
And they decided they going to hunt.
Hunt deer or moose.
So they went.
Went on the mountain.
They got a pack horse.
They riding two horses.
And they got some grub and tent
    and they got a pack horse.
And they went up.
And they went way up on the mountain
    and they happen to come in the place
        where kind of a slough, kind of a wet ground, like.
Mostly water, but not lake.
There's a lot of water.
They kind of a swamp.

224

Swampy ground.
Then they come to that place
  and then they said to one another,
      "That place is too wet.
        Maybe we go to some certain place where it's dry.
        And we put a camp there.
        And it's not late yet.
        We can unload the packhorse.
        Then we tie 'em.
        Then we ride.
        Then we make a circle, hunting.
        But when it's late, then we come back.
        And our camp, we left 'em right here."

They didn't hear nothing.
Then they went out.
They left the packhorse.
Unload 'em and left 'em there.
And they went around for quite a ways.
Take 'em about couple of hours or more.
But when they come to their camp,
  they get near and then they could hear that bird.
That's the cranes.
Lots of 'em.

And when they left the camp
  and this one,
      they arrive in that swampy
        and then they're going to stay there
          for overnight, these birds.
So when they get to the camp
  they could hear that not far from,
      like the camp was here,
        and just about this far as his place
          in the swampy.
Then they make a lot of noise, you know.
They could heard 'em.
So they build a fire
  and they cook some supper and then they eat.
Then one of 'em, he says,
  "That bird, it must have been hungry.

They make so much noise.
They musta been hungry."
And the other one says,
  "No, they couldn't be hungry.
  They musta been happy.
  They musta find something to eat where they are.
  That's why they were making a noise.
  They mighta been happy."
And the other one say,
  "No, they mighta be, they hungry.
  That's why they make a lot of noise."

So in a little while, they finish their supper.
Then he's got a fire and he's sitting there.
Then he could see somebody come
  from where that lot of noise.
The light, the fire light, you know, for quite a ways.
Then it comes to the light.
Then they could see two of 'em.
Looks like two man they were coming.
They just watch.
They never said nothing.
They just watch till they comes to the other side of the fire.
See?
They were sitting on this side of the fire.
Then these two men, they comes from the other side.
And the same.
They looked like a bird or looks like a person.
It's kind of a half and half, the way it looks like.
Then he stand there a little while and told 'em,
  "You guys think that we musta been hungry
    over there in our camp,
      and that's where we make a noise.
    That's what this fella thinks.
    But this one here, but maybe we're happy."

See?
They told 'em what they think
  and what they say.
And they never say nothing.
But they told 'em,

"Just because you say that,
    and we think you guys were hungry.
  You guys come here to see if you can find some food.
  And you never did find 'em.
  Not yet.
  Maybe you guys were hungry,
    but we aren't.
  We got a lot of food.
  We come here to tell you that,
    and we going to give you some food from our food."

Well, what they got to say?
They didn't say nothing.
And each one of them,
  they had something in the roll.
Like if you roll the canvas,
  something in the canvas and you roll 'em
    and you had 'em in your arm.
So they give 'em to one of 'em and says,
  "This is yours."
And the other one,
  the other one give 'em one roll and tell 'em,
  "You just leave it there.
   In the morning you undo this roll
     and break 'em out and you can see food.
   Then you eat that food.
   And you eat all you want.
   Then they'll be still there.
   Then you roll 'em again just like I have 'em there.
   Then you keep it.
   Whenever you hungry just unroll 'em.
   Then you eat.
   Then you'll never eat 'em all.
   You'll eat all you want and it can be still there.
   And it's no use for you guys to hunt.
   You take that.
   Tomorrow you go home.
   When you get to your people,
     you call all your people together,
       then give 'em some of this food.
   Then they can eat all they want

      and still the same.
    Never eat 'em all."

That's what this bird told 'em.
So, they tell 'em,
    "That's what we want to give you.
    Then we go back.
    But if somebody ask you
      'How did you get this?'
        when you unroll 'em and feed the people,
          when they ask you, 'How did you get that?,'
            don't say.
    Don't say that we give you that.
    Don't tell.
    If you tell 'em, somebody,
      it'll be no more.
    But if you don't tell 'em,
      you can have that for the rest of your time.
    And you could feed people.
    Doesn't matter how many.
    But once you tell people how you get it,
      it'll be no more."

All right.
The next morning, early in the morning,
  and they could hear this bird taking off.
Fly up and go.
But when the sun come up
  and they get their horses,
    and they go back because they got the food already.
There's no use hunt.

So when they get back to their people for a couple days
  and ask 'em,
    "You guys suppose to be hunting,
      but you come back with nothing."
    "Yeah, we got some food,
      but maybe we call the people
        and we can feed 'em."
So they call the people and all the people come.
So this other one, they unroll his food

and the other one did, like two places.
Then there was a lot of food when they undone.
Then all the people,
  they eat that food
    and they eat all they can and all they want.
Still there!
Never eat 'em all!
They roll 'em and put it away.
For a long time they do that.
They eat that and sometimes,
  once in a while, they call the people
    and the people come and eat.
But I don't know what kind of food, though,
  that's one thing.
But they suppose to be good food.
And one of 'em, he got a wife
  in different direction, in different country, like.
Like far away.
So he go over there and he stay over there
  and they seems to go apart.
That's not his brother, but just his friend.
But they live together, like, all the time,
  but this time the one of 'em got a wife
    and then they move for quite a ways.
And one of 'em, the one that say,
  "That bird must have been hungry"
    when it make too much noise,
      he's the one that got a wife far away.
And he go over there.
But while he was over there
  and the people asked him
    "How did you get this food? Who give it to you?"
Finally he tell.
He tell all about.
Next time he unroll that, no more!
And the other one the same.
He didn't tell, but once the other one, he tell,
  the both of 'em, no more that food.

That's not too long ago.
So that stories, it went from north

and far as where I was and I heard that stories,
and I don't know if that was true or not,
but that's the way I heard it.
So that's the end for that.

Breaking Bones at a Stickgame

Some stickgame players have a lot of power. One man surprises
the people during a game.

Did you ever see stickgame player?
And they had a bone.
They make the things out of a bone.
Like that, you know.
They just about this size.
They hold 'em there.
That's bones.
Solid bone.
It was made out of bone.
They fire 'em a little and then they shape 'em, the bone.
Hard.
Just as hard as this.
And they hold that.
And one in here.
Then, some power person,
   he pointed to this hand.
And that was the one, if he get that,
   the other one, he lose.
But, he's got a power enough to squeeze that bone
   and smash it all to pieces.
When the other one point, he still hold it.
When he let them go, just drop in small pieces.
Broke, the pieces.
Just like you hammer 'em with a hammer.
That bone.
Just hold 'em and just squeeze it.
And let go and they all drop in pieces.
So that shows that he was a power man
   in their hands or anyplace.
Just to show the others he's a power man.

They hold that bone.
Nobody can do that.
Doesn't matter how hard you squeeze the bone,
   it will never broke.
But the power man,
   he squeeze it and broke it.
So, I didn't see that,
   but I heard in the stories,
     and whoever, some of the people,
       they seen that
         and they tell the stories about them.

So that shows, some people, they got a power.
Strong power.
Better than the others.
The others, they might have a power
   but still they couldn't do that.
That's another.
There's a lot of different ways in the power.

Indian Doctor

A woman announces at a winter dance that she has power to doctor people. When a man is seriously stabbed a short while later, they go and get this woman to work on him. It is her first doctoring, but her power is strong.

There's one woman down in Okanogan Washington,
   just the other side of Omak.
She put up a *shnay-WUM** herself, you know.
Susan Joseph, her name was.
And they put up a *shnay-WUM.*
And some other people, they goes in there
   and they have the *shnay-WUM* for one winter.
Second winter, they went and make a *shnay-WUM,*
   but in the third winter they had a *shnay-WUM,*
     she put up the *shnay-WUM* herself,
       alone.
And when they finish, they give away blankets,
   and clothes and buckskin, you know, and stuff like that.

When she finish, she says to the people,
   "I'm going to tell you what I'm going to be from now on."
She says,
   "If anybody got hurt, and he got blood inside of him,
     supposing if somebody got stabbed with knife,
     or somebody got shot with gun,
     or somebody fall off from a horse,
     or from something, and get hurt,
       as long as they got injured, let me know.
   See what I'll do."
All right.

---

*The *shnay-WUM* is the traditional Okanagan winter dance ceremony which is held annually by some families for spiritual healing and renewal.

The people remember that.
In winter she say that.
That summer, in the month of June,
 and one fella, he got stabbed.
Someone stabbed him in the belly here with a knife, you know,
 cut him open.
Then, the other people they says,
 "That Susan, she says she is going to be good for the people
  that get hurt. Go get her."

So they went and get her.
She was at home and she see somebody in the morning,
 about eight o'clock in the morning,
  somebody come, come down the hill pretty fast,
   leading a horse.

They come and tell Susan,
 "I coming to get you.
  My brother got hurt.
  He was stabbed with a knife.
  Maybe he's going to die.
  Badly stabbed. Big opening here."
 "All right, I go."

So she got a special dress.
She can put that on to do the work.
She made that dress and keep 'em,
 never wear 'em.
Only when she go to work, she put them on.
Just like the priests, you know,
 the priests, put them on for the mass.
Something like that.
And then she went.
They got to go up the hill.
Kinda sandy ground and the horses, they gallop.
But they couldn't gallop fast enough up the hill,
 and kinda sandy.
They going slow.
Then, the horses kind of played out till they get up to the top.
It's not steep, you know, but it's uphill.
When they get to the top, and she says to this man,

whoever come and get her, she says to him,
  "When we get to the top of the hill, we turn off the road,
    and we get off and set down there for a while.
      I want to smoke."

So, this man, he think,
  Well, why did she have to stop there to smoke?
  My brother, he going to die.
  She should get there right away.
He think, but he didn't say it, but he think in his heart.

So they turn off the road, stop, and they get off their horses.
And this man hold the horses,
  and she got a pipe,
    a handmade pipe, you know.
They make 'em out of stone.
And she fill up with tobacco.
She have to cut the plug.
Hard tobacco.
It's been in a plug.
And she cut that with a knife,
  and cut 'em and cut 'em and cut 'em.
Then she put 'em in the pipe.
Then the kinnikinnik, she smash that and put them mixed,
  then light and then she smoked in the pipe.
And it takes a while to do that before she smoke.
And this man, he think,
  What the heck do we have to smoke here for?
He never said, but he think that.

When she finish smoking, then she put that away
  and she says to him,
    "Don't you think that.
     When I smoke, I'm looking at that man
      and now I know I'm going to get there
        and I know I'm going to get him to be all right.
    That's why I smoke.
    If I don't smoke I don't know
     if I'm going to get him to be all right or not.
    But when I smoke, I know.
    Now, we go."

She know what he thinks, but she didn't say.
She's Indian doctor.
She knows that by her power.

So, they got on, and went and get to the place.
There was a camp, bunch of people,
   lot of camp.
Quite a few camp along the creek there.
They were camping there.
They were supposed to be go to church there,
   they call that Corpus Christi.
And they go to church about a couple days,
   the priest, you know.
That's why all the people gather there.
Some people were drinking, you know.
They always do.
Some people go to the church and some people drink.
They always do that.

So, there's a lot of people there.
The Indian doctor, she come,
   and she see that man that get hurt,
      they pile up the blanket and pillows
         and they lay him there just kind of half sitting,
            lay there.
Just like you lay on that chair and sit back, like that.
And quite a little ways,
   when they get off the saddlehorse, you know in the cabin,
      get off the saddle horse and stepped on the ground.
You know, if you get off the saddlehorse
   and you step on the ground first
      before you pull your other foot off the stirrup,
         step on the ground.
Just as soon as she hit the ground with her foot,
   and up comes her song,
      come out.
And she started to sing loud, right away.
Then, she turn,
   and she walk towards the injured man kinda slow.
Walk slow,
   and when she get from about here to that wall there

and she stop.
Sing there for a while and she put her hand like that.
Put it like that,
   and sing her song.
And some of the people, they all watching.
Turn around and look at the one lady and says,
   "Get me water. Get me water right from the creek."
And the creek is quite a little ways down.
And this lady, she pick up a bucket
   and run down to the creek
      and get fresh water.
And she come and she says,
   "Put 'em in the basin."
And they take the basin, and they put this water in the basin
   and they set it right alongside of 'em.
And they said that injured man,
   he was laying like from here to the corner over there,
      just about that far, laying,
And she said,
   "You pick up the water."
   "I can't see."
   "Pick up the water."
She says,
   "I throw the water to 'em.
      When I throw the water to 'em it's just like little balls."
And it hit him right in the forehead.

Then again she sing awhile
   and get another one.
Then she throw that one.
Who can hold the water and throw 'em?
Nobody.

Then, after that, and she walked over there,
   and she get to that man.
This man was lay against the pillow,
   the blanket, high, you know,
      laying there.
And she kind of sit alongside of him.
And she put her hands like that.
See, there's hole here, like that.

237

Put her hands like that,
  and then she put it, she don't put 'em like that,
    about four inches away from her mouth,
      and about four inch away from the body.
Then she "ssssss,"
  she suck the blood,
    and they could never see the blood come through here
      because her hand was about four inch away from her mouth,
        and four inch away from the body.
You could never see the blood come through there
  in the open.
Then she turn around and spit in the water.
Just blood.
Black blood.
Then sing her song, sing her song for a while.
Same way — "sssssss,"
Spit, and the blood was just straight blood.
On the third time, the blood was just kind of a yellow.
She said,
  "No more."
She suck that blood out of him
  because if that blood builds up inside
    then it comes to the heart and die.
Says, "All right, that's all.
      I go down and get some medicine
        and fix the medicine for you,
          and then you okay."

She went down to the creek herself.
Get some of them willow.
She get the bark off the willow,
  and she kind of smash that and mix 'em with the water
    and wet it, you know.
And she put them on the cut, you know, on the open.
Put them on and wrap 'em up with the handkerchief or something
Said,
  "You keep that, and you lay there for a while.
    When the sun goes about halfways from noon to sunset,
      you get up and you walk around.
    In the morning, just as soon as the sun comes
      out from the mountain,

238

and you get up and walk around.
And after that you'll be all right."

That man, he get better.
That's the first one, she did that work.
But another time, I watching 'em.
I was there.
She suck the blood the same way.
Just like that.
And I was stand right alongside of her.
And I could never see the blood come.
But she spit blood.
It's pretty hard to believe that.

PART FOUR:
WORLD UNSETTLED
THE AGE OF THE WHITE MAN

Harry at Coyote rock, near his old home at Paul Creek, 1985.
Coyote left his bait here while he fished.

Fur Traders

They tell the Indian to get fur.
Put in trap and get fur.
Then they buy that and trade 'em.
They trade, you know.
They cheating the Indian at that time.

See the gun?
See this gun here?
See?
They put this gun,
   they stand 'em on the ground like that.
Well, the gun is higher.
In those days the gun is long.

And he stand that gun.
Then they pile the hides from the ground.
Build 'em right up even with the gun.

"All right, you take the gun. I take the hides."

And the gun, it was only about $30.
And then the hide, it was about $900.

See?
They traded that way.
That was wrong.

Captive in an English Circus

A man from the Similkameen Valley goes to prison in New Westminster for killing a man. One night he is secretly abducted and taken on a long journey.

This is about George Jim.
He belongs to Ashnola Band, George Jim.
Those days, I had it written down — 1886.
No, I mean 1887.
That's one year I'm out there.
That's supposed to be in the 1886
  instead of 1887.
That time, 1886,
  the people, Indians from Penticton,
    all the Okanagan Indians,
      they were some from Similkameen,
        and they all move to where Oroville is now
          in the month of August,
            about the last week in the month of August.
And they all get together in Oroville.
And that's when the salmon coming up.
The salmon comes up, you know, from way down.
They come up on the Columbia River
  and they come up on the Okanogan, some.
And some of them go up, they split up there.
Some of them go up the Columbia River.
But some of them, they coming up on the Okanogan River.
They had a good place for catching them there in Oroville.
Kind of shallow.
Only a small river.

So the people moved over there.
They stay there.
Put in a camp.

There is no town there yet.
There was some white people,
  they got two or three houses there.
Not many.
Then they get the salmon.
They get the salmon for,
  could be about a week or ten days.
Then the salmon keep going and go by.
They come to Osoyoos Lake
  and they follow Osoyoos Lake
    and then they come to Okanogan River again
      and they keep going to Okanagan Falls.
They can never go any farther than Okanagan Falls.
There's a dam there.
That's as far as the salmon can go.

These Indian, when they run out of salmon,
  they know the salmon, they go by.
So they move.
Follow the salmon.
Then they come to Okanagan Falls.
Then the salmon, they can't go no more.
They were there.
They can get salmon.
Some of them died in the water
  and get bad, you know, get spoiled.
Then they quit.
When they get together at Falls,
  there's a lot of Indians and they put in a camp.
Some of them, they play stickgame.
They kind of celebrate.
But still some of them get the salmon
  at night or the daytime.
And some of them get whiskey from someplace,
  from Penticton, I guess, or somewhere.
And they drink.

And this time,
  that Jim,
    supposed to be a big man, stout man.
And he's a funny looking man.

245

He's got short legs,
  but he's pretty wide in the shoulders.
And he's got big hips.
Kinda tough-looking man.
And he was.
He's a strong man.

Then there was a white man
  that lived there at Okanagan Falls.
And he's got an Indian woman from Penticton.
And they got some children,
  maybe one or two.
And this white man, his name, Shattleworth.

A lot of people drinking, you know.
And then George Jim, and Shattleworth, and some others,
  they drinking at night,
    and then they fighting.
But this time, that Shattleworth,
  he got beat badly by George Jim.
George Jim, he beat him almost till death.
Then, some of the boys, they stopped him and grab him.
Because he's strong, it takes a few men to hold him.
Then they take the man who's wounded.
They take him to the camp.
They laid him in the camp.
He's hurt very bad.
He's got a broken ribs
  and he was hurt in the head, you know.
Quite a few cuts.
With a club, you know, he hit him in the head with a club
  and then he cut the skin, you know, by the club.
Not knife, but the club.
Then he kicked him in the ribs
  and his ribs were broken inside.
And then some of that bone,
  they must have gone to the lungs.
Could be.

He thought,
  I hurt him badly

and I might as well kill him.

So, who's going to stop him?
He's a strong man.
He went to the teepee.
Bunch of women in there,
   maybe two or three old men
      and maybe five women, old women.

So he come there and he says,
   "How's that Shattleworth?
   I'm going to kill him if he's alive yet."
And these people told him,
   "He's dead.
   He died.
   Already died."

And they covered him with a white blanket.
He lay on the bed
   and they cover him, all his head.
And he looked like he was dead all right
   because he was covered with a white cloth.
They tell him,
   "You better stay away.
   He died.
   He dead already."

All right, he go away.

But he didn't die, that Shattleworth.
After that he was living for about seven or eight months.
But he died just from getting beat
   because the way I see, maybe the ribs they were broken
      and maybe some, they go to the lungs.
But if not go to the lungs,
   the ribs they be heal up.
He wouldn't die.
But this one here, it's bad.
Maybe it goes in the lung,
   the bone, the broken rib.

247

But anyway, George got away.
And then they report that to the policeman
  because this Shattleworth, he's a white man
    and he's got an Indian wife.
And it was reported to the police.
But the police, they couldn't get him.
Kinda scared of him because Jim,
  he's got a revolver on his hip all the time,
    and yet he's a strong man.
And the policeman, they kinda scared of him.
They just let him go.
They look for a chance to sneak to him and then get him.

So Jim, he stay away for quite a while,
  for almost one year.
About eleven months after he did that,
  that was next August and somebody, they cheat him.
Then they got him.
And he been around to Ashnola and down to Chopaka.
But he always keep away from the policeman.
They go over there and look for him,
  but they're scared of him.
They always around there but nobody get him.
He hide in the daytime in the hillside.
At night he goes to the Indian camp
  and sometimes he didn't.

Then, there was one boy, eleven years old.
And he make a lunch,
  a big lunch for Jim.
Then he told that boy,
  he told an old man,
    "You take that boy
      and show him the place
        where he can leave that lunch for Jim.
      And tell him what he's going to do.
      And tell him what he's got to say if somebody met him."
That old man used to take the lunch,
  but he a little afraid
    maybe the policeman or some man
      might think the old man

must have take a lunch to that wanted man.
But if the boy,
  he give him a gun, you know,
    a 22-gun, you know,
      to shoot the grouse.
And he tell him,
  "If somebody come and met you,
    if they ask you what you're doing here,
      you tell 'em,
        'I'm hunting, hunting for grouse,
          willow grouse, or rabbit, or something like that.'"

Then, he's got bags on his shoulders.
  "When I get a grouse I can put it in there."
But that's where he had the lunch.
And he showed him where he can take the lunch
  and where he can leave it.
There was a big stone
  and there was kind of hollow underneath the stone.
That was kind of a shade.
In the daytime he could put the lunch there.

But this man is up on the hill.
He could be watching him.
When it gets dark,
  this man will come down and take the lunch
    and go up the hill again.
That's Jim.
So the old man, he show the boy
  and tell all about what to do and what to say.
And he can take the lunch every once in awhile,
  every two days,
    because they make a big lunch at a time.

But not long after that,
  that was in the month of August, could be,
    because they say that choke cherries were ripe.
They don't know if it was August or September those days.
Now I can figure myself.
When they say it's choke cherries time,
  choke cherries, they ripe,

choke cherries they ripe in the month of August.
I know that.
That could be in August.
Then he was there for quite a while.

And the road gang, they building a road.
And they call it McCurdy place.
And after that, they call it,
  I forget the new man that lived there.
Anyway, McCurdy place,
  that's the first man that lived there.
McCurdy for about a mile
  and the river it's curved like that.
Kind of bent.
And that's where they camp, the road gang,
  they had a camp there.
Those days wherever they can build a road,
  if it's far away from town,
    they can move camp.
They got to have a camp there.
But nowadays, the workers,
  they can go from town.
It don't matter how far.
They don't put no camp.
But those days they got a camp.
They use horses, you know,
  scraper and plough to make a grade.
And they had a camp there,
  the road gang, the bunch of them.
And they had a cookhouse and a cook.
Bunch of men workers.
And there was a trail,
  but they widen out that trail to be a wagon road.
That was in 1887 then.
That's a long time ago.
No highway those days.

So the road gang was there.
And one of these boys, like the boss,
  maybe, the foreman, you know,
    he has to ride the horse.

No car those days,
  no motorcycle,
    no bicycle,
      no nothing.
Only saddle horse.
You know that.

Then these men
  they go to Fairview.
That's a town, you know.
Mine town.
Their head boss is there.
Government.

All right.
They went over there to see him
  and come back.
So he went over there
  and then in the afternoon, he come back from Fairview.
He went over there in the morning.
In the afternoon he come back from there.

And this George Jim,
  he took a horse and ride him around by Nighthawk.
Then he must have gone by Oroville or somewhere.
But he come back
  and he come back where that Osoyoos Road is now.

You remember when we come up there?
And I showed you, "Here is the old road?"
But now the highway is above the old road.

So Jim, he come on that road.
And the other one,
  that man who goes to Fairview,
    he takes the trail like from Fairview.
And they met at the top, just above Spotted Lake.

When we were at Spotted Lake
  and you took pictures, I and him?
And I told you, the old road, it's higher up there?

Yeah, that's where they meet,
  this man from Fairview.
He go by Spotted Lake.
And Jim was coming on the road
  and they met there.
Then, because Jim, he's a "wanted man,"
  it was written in the government office,
    his name and how he look like and all that.
And all the white people knew that
  even if they never seen him before.
But as soon as they see him,
  they can tell that was the "wanted man."

So this man, one of the government men,
  the one that goes to Fairview,
    soon as he met him,
      he knew he was the one.
There was a reward, you know,
  because whoever catch him is going to get paid.
Then he said to George,
  they go together and they talk
    and they make a good friend to one another,
      and they are good friend
        and it's getting late in the afternoon.
Finally they rode together
  and they're getting close to the camp.
Then, it's just about supper-time then.
And this white man, he tell Jim,
  "You better come with me to the camp.
  Then you can eat there.
  Eat supper.
  Now, it's just about supper-time."
He tell him,
  "I am one of the bosses in that camp,
    so you come with me
      and you stay there
        and after supper you can go."
And Jim, he says,
  "No, I better keep going.
  I can stop someplace in some of them Indians."
  "Oh no. You better come.

You eat here. You'll be all right."

But you know, he figure,
  when he get there,
    he figure he can tell the other boys right away
      and that was their judge to catch him.

So anyway,
  George, he must have been hungry or something
    because he stop there
      and he went with that man.
And he tie up his horse.
Then, I think this white man,
  the one that's with him,
    he must have tell the other ones right away.
And then he didn't know.

And then,
  one of the working man,
    big man, strong man,
      he take the apron and he put it here.
He's not a waiter.
He's not a cook.
He's one of the ploughmen.
But he puts the apron on so he looks like a waiter, cook.
Long table
  and he takes the grub
    and he move over there
      and he goes back and gets some more.

And Jim was sitting there
  and he wanted to sit on the other side against the tent wall.
But they tell him,
  "You can sit here.
   Already the boys are over there."

He didn't like to sit there because it's open.

So this waiter goes by him
  on his back two, three times.
And then I guess these other boys,

253

nobody know,
   they might get a club and then they hide it.
When the waiter gets over the other end of the table
  and he give him that club.
Then he come back.
That was the fourth time or the fifth time
  when he go by George's back.

Then this time when he go by there,
  and George was watching all the time.
He always watching.
But finally he quieted down
  and he eat.
And he's got a revolver on his hip, you know.

And when this waiter go by him,
  down it went on the back of his head
    and George just drop!
And he knocked out
  and drop off the chair.
And all the men are just on him, you know.
Bunch of men, three or four men,
  they just right on him.
And they get the rope
  and they tie his arms
    and they tie his feet.
Before he come to, he's already tied up.
He can't do nothing.
They take his gun away from him.

Then they sent one of the boys to Fairview for the policeman
  after supper, after six o'clock.
Then, whoever they went from there to Fairview,
  that's about ten or fifteen miles,
    they get there and tell the police
      and then the policemen come.
When the policemen gets there
  and they handcuff him,
    put the handcuffs on him.
Then, nothing he can do after they got the handcuffs.
They take the ropes off his feet

254

and then they tell him,
  "Get on you horse."
And these policemen,
  they come on horses,
    the two of them.
Then they lead him
  and they tie his feet with a rope under the belly
    so he could never jump off.
They got handcuffs, iron handcuffs.
He can't get away.
So they lead him to Fairvew
  and then they put him in jail.

Because the one, he beat Shattleworth.
He did.
After the six or seven months after he was beat,
  he died.
He's a murderer anyway.

So, they held him in that jail for a while
  and they had a trial there once or twice.
Then they take him to Penticton.
There was another courthouse there.
Just small.
They held him there awhile
  and then they took him to Kamloops.
There must have been a little court in Vernon those days.
But Kamloops.
Then they had him there for a while
  and then they got a sentence seven years.
Only seven years.
Take him to Westminster.
And the railroad drives into Westminster in 1886.
And they already had a railroad right in Vancouver.

And Mr. Jim,
  they sent him from Kamloops on the railroad to Westminster.
And then they had him in that penitentiary.
And he was in there three years.
Supposed to be seven years and then he'll come out.
That's his sentence.

Seven years.

He was in jail three years
   and one night towards morning,
      about two o'clock in the morning then
         because all the cells, you know,
            whoever's in the cell, maybe one or two,
            the policeman lock 'em.
Then, in the morning they could open 'em.
Unlock 'em.
But Jim was locked.
All alone in one cell.
But towards morning,
   about two o'clock in the morning,
      somebody open that.
They got a key,
   open the door,
      and they come in.
There's three of them — policemen.
They got the clothes, uniform — guards.
Those days, the policemen,
   they haven't got no uniform.
But the guards, they got some kind of a uniform.

So, the three of them come in.
And Jim, he wake up.
Still in bed.
And told him,
   "Jim, you get up and put your clothes on.
    We come and get you."

I'm not sure if it was three.
I think it's only two.
But the driver, that makes three.
They got a driver on the buggy out there.
But these two,
   they're both guards,
     go in and tell Jim,
        "You dress up and we come and get you.
       There's a buggy outside with a driver.
       You get on the buggy

and we all get on and we go to Vancouver.
Early in the morning,
   the train is going to leave Vancouver.
We got to go on the train.
We move you.
There was one jail a long long way from here.
We move you.
You're going to be over at that jail.
Long ways from here.
You leave this place."

Well what can he say,
   because this is the policeman, guard, you know.
He has to do whatever they tell him.
All right, he dress up and he went out.
There was a buggy there
   and he get on the buggy
      and they all get on the buggy
         and they go to Vancouver early in the morning.

At that time they got a different time.
Now, they leave there eight o'clock in the evening from Vancouver.
But at that time it might have been in the morning.
Might be four o'clock in the morning
   or something like that.

Anyway,
   early in the morning they get on the train
      and they went.
And they going all day and all night
   and all day and all night again.
And Mr. Jim, he thinks,
   By God, that was a long way.
   Where did they take me?
   I wonder where they take me.

They take him into where they eat, you know,
   on the train.
And he got a chance to ask the waiter.
I guess the policemen who look after him, they went back,
   and just only himself.

And he asked the waiter,
  and the waiter told him,
    "They take you to Halifax.
      Then there, you're going to take the boat
        from Halifax to England."

So, he find that out,
  but what has he got to say?
So anyway, they get him to Halifax.
Then they told him,
  "We're going to be here for a while.
    We're waiting for the boat."
Because those days
  it takes the boat a month to go over the sea to England.
One month.
But now it's only about four days.
So they wait there about four or five days.
Then the boat came.
Then they put him in the boat,
  the whole bunch.
These two, they always along with him,
  the same man.

So, he mention that.
He see one Indian in England
  and he told him,
    this Indian from Enderby,
      not Indian altogether,
        he's a half-breed,
          but he speak in Okanagan.
So, he says in his stories that he went on the water.
He could see the mountains, the ground,
  for one week and no more.
Two weeks,
  never see nothing but water.
Then he see again a little ridge.
Little ground.
One week and then they landed.
Then from there
  they took him on the buggy
    or on the train or something for quite a ways.

Then they leave him there.
But not in jail no more.
They give him a good house,
 a good big house,
  big room,
   good bed.
They feed him good
 and then they kept him.
They watch him all the time.
But once in awhile they took him
 and put him on the train
  and they went away.
They stay away for two or three months
 and then come back.
That was his home place.
In two months or more,
 they come back to England
  and they stay there for two or three weeks,
   maybe one month,
    then they took him to another direction.
That's in European somewhere.

They took him everywhere for show.
Whenever they get somewhere
 and there'd be a big forum
  and table or something.
Then they tell him to get up there
 and walk around there.
Then, the people in the big room,
 big house chock full of people,
  and he watching them.
And these people, they pay.
Pay money to see that Indian.
There is no Indian in Europe at that time.
Only him.

So the white people, they make money out of him.
And he was there four years.

And this man from Enderby,
 he's a half-breed.

259

His name, Charlie.
Charlie Harvie, his name.
He talks in Okanagan.
He's half-breed.
And he don't say,
  but I think myself he must be in the army,
    that Charlie,
      because he went and he get to England.
Then he come back from England
  and he came home to Enderby.
And when he got home,
  he said when he was in England,
    he said, there's a big bunch of boys,
      all young boys just like he was,
        just like his age.
Bunch of them and they were there.

So one of these boys told him,
  asked him where he come from.
And he said he came from the Okanagan, British Columbia.
Okanagan.
Then, he told him,
  "There was a man not far from here,
    he is supposed to come from Okanagan, British Columbia.
  He is supposed to speak in your language.
  Maybe we should take you over there
    and then you can see that man."

Then, he said,
  "No, I don't like to go because,"
  (see, he's got a boss, he must be an army man),
  "My boss they may not like it that way."
So, the other boss says,
  "Your boss, he's not going to know that.
  We take you over there.
  We're not going to tell your boss.
  You're going to see that man."

All right.
So they went.
The boys took him over there.

Then they get to that place
  and they go in to where that Jim was.
That's his house.
Then the boys told him,
  "This man, he speak in your language."
Then the both of them started to speak in Okanagan.

Not only one.
He went over there two or three times
  to see him and visit him
    for quite a while.

And Jim,
  he told him all about what they have done
    and so on.
And then they took him from Westminster
  and they took him on the train a long ways
    and they put him on the boat for one month.
Then they had him there.
  "Then they take me out from here a long ways.
    I don't know which way,
      but they take me out a long ways.
    Wherever I stop, a lot of people get in there.
    Then they make me walk around on the boards.
    High.
    Then I walk around and all the people look at me.
    Then I go.
    We go to another place.
    Then we go to another place.
    A lot of places.
    In one month or two months
      we come back.
    And this is my home place."

But he says,
  "Charlie, when you get back to British Columbia,
    you can go from Enderby to Ashnola."
Right in Ashnola he's got aunt and he's got uncle.
And he said to Charlie,
  "You could tell my uncle and my aunt
    to make a business,

261

to see if they can come and get me.
They got a lot of money.
They got a lot of cattle.
They got enough money.
They should come and get me.
In another way they can talk to the Indian agent.
And then the Indian agent can contact to Ottawa,
   to the Indian Affairs.
Then, whoever they is coming to get me,
   their fare can be paid that way.
But maybe they'll have a little money with them anyway.
But my people, they're well-off.
They should do that and come and get me."

So Charlie, he said,
   "I will when I get home."

And about a year after that,
   Charlie came back.
Come back to Enderby.
He stay there almost one year after that and he come back.
And then he ride on the saddle horse all the way to Ashnola.
Then he see that John, his name was,
   and Mary.
They are cousins.
That's Jim's aunt, that Mary,
   and his uncle, John.
He told them all about it
   to contact the Indian agent and to Ottawa
      and all that.
And he said,
   "If you want me, I can be with you,"
      because he can speak in English, you know.

But these Indians, they couldn't understand.
They don't know.
In another way, they don't like it.

They say,
   "He should not pay for our fare
      because that's a lot of money."

They figure they could pay for their own fare
   but it takes a lot of money.
And they could never understand about the contact
   so they could get paid their fare from the Indian affairs.
Charlie told them,
   but they couldn't understand.
Charlie, he was waiting around,
   and he said,
      "I go home, but if you need me, I come back and help you,
         or else I can go with you for interpreter over there
            to get that man back."

But they just dismissed.
No more.
They never get him.

But, before they find out he was alive yet
   at the time when they took Jim from Westminster,
      take him away,
         then they rode from the jail to John.
He was a chief, you know.
And they told John that
   "Jim was in jail here
      but he died and we bury him."

But he not die.
They lie.
They take him away.

So they think, his people,
   they just got to know he died and that's all.
But they decided they should come and get the body.
Take it out and bring him home.
So they did.
They come, that John and Mary and some others.
They got an interpreter, you know,
   who can speak in English.
Then they come on horseback with the packhorses to Hope.
Then they talk to the people in Hope
   and they tell them,
      "You can't leave your horses here.

263

There's no feed for the horses.
You have to go to Chilliwack
   and then you can put your horses in there with the Indians.
There's all kinds of feed there for horses.
And then you can take the boat from Chilliwack to Westminster."

So, they did.
They did get to Westminster
  and then they go to the jail office
     and they tell 'em,
          "We're coming to get George Jim.
          He's already buried here."
So, they said,
          "Yeah, we talk to one another.
          We'll see.
          Just wait awhile, a couple of days."

Then, they talk to one another
  and I guess they find out what to say about him.
Then they say,
  "All right, we know.
   This is the one right there in the graveyard.
   We can dig him.
   We dig him out and we clean 'em and we change the coffin.
   Then you guys can take him on the boat as far as Chilliwack
      and then you could put him on the packhorse."

Well, it's in a box
  because they could pack the horse on each side of something.
Then they could put the box crossways
  all the ways from Chilliwack to Ashnola.
Then they did that
  and they take him out and clean him
     and put medicine on him
        so he wouldn't be smell.
Change the coffin and seal it
  and told them not to open it.
   "Don't open it
      because we give him medicine.
      But in the box he's not cold.
      They might be kinda smell,

by the time you get it over there,
        not to open 'em."

All right, they bring 'em
  and they never open 'em.
But when they get him to Ashnola,
  then, whoever they were there,
      and they tell 'em,
        "We should open 'em.
          We should make sure if that was him."
Well, these other people said,
    "If he's going to be smelly, that don't matter.
      Open 'em.
      We want to see."
So, they break it open and they looked at 'em.
    "That's not Jim. That was a Chinaman."
Kinda stout Chinaman.
He must have been in jail.

They can't take him back, so they bury him there.
They were around there for a while
  and they thought maybe they make a mistake over there.
      "We better go again to get Jim.
        They might mistake.
        Maybe Jim is still there."

They went again
  and they get there
    and they told 'em,
        "This is not Jim you give us.
        This is a Chinaman."
        "By gosh, that's too bad.
        We made a mistake.
        We know that.
        We find that out,
            but you fellas are gone.
        George is there.
        Now that you've come back,
            we can take him out and clean him
              and you can take him away.
        Take him home."

265

They do the same thing.
Dug him out, clean him, put medicine on him
   and changed the box, and tell him not to open it.

So, they bring him,
   and that was the second time.
From Westminster to Chilliwack.
Then, they packed him from Chilliwack to Ashnola.
When they get there,
   whoever they were home tell 'em,
     "We got to open 'em, see,
       to make sure if it was Jim.
      Maybe another Chinaman."

Anyhow, they open 'em.
They looked at him
  and he was a negro boy.
A small man too.

Well, they bury him there.
But there's no use to go back and get George.

And George is not dead.
They take him away.

Then later on, a few years after that,
  and Charlie Harvie come back from England.
Then he ride over there and he tell them about it.

Long time, quite a few years after that,
  and then they find out
    George Jim, he's not dead.
He's alive yet, but he's in England.

So, that's the end of that story.

To Hell and Back

*A man murders four men for their gold. Many many years later,
his crime catches up with him before — and after — he dies.*

That's not too long ago.
That's about,
   it was in 1886 when that happens.
1886 at that year when that happens.
Not Spence's Bridge, but this side a bit.
In another way they call it Skookum Spring.
Skookum Spring, that's in another way they call 'em
   15-Mile Creek.
That's 15 miles from Spence's Bridge
   where that Antony Joe lives.
And where he live and up to the bench.
There were some other houses there.
That's the place.
But from there straight across the river
   on top of the mountain, not very high.

And this man, his name,
   he got two Indian name.
I don't know.
He mighta be baptized.
May not, those days.
But anyway, he got two names in Indian.
They call him Ta-POO-low.
That means,
   supposing if you turn that into English word,
      that means "frozen ground harder."
That's one name
   and the other name they call 'em Shil-ka-CHOOT.
That's a Thompson word.

I don't know what that means.*
And the other word were Thompson word,
   but I know what it means.

So this man, he's kinda husky man.
And seems to be good man, but he don't like to work.
But he want money.
There's a lot of people like that.
Lot of people, they can't work for money
   but they want the money.
They want to get the money somehow for nothing.
Steal it or tell some kind of a word
   and they could get it for nothing.
A lot of people like that even today.
And this man was like that.
Ta-POO-low, he don't want to work for money,
   but he want to have money.
So in the other way,
   everybody think he good man.
It look like good man,
   but he not good in another way.

At those days white people,
   they call it a gold rush at everywhere.
They found the gold kinda often at anyplace.
And lot of 'em gold mine were found along that way.
Along Spence's Bridge and down the river to Hope
   and all over the Cariboo and all those places.
They found the gold mine.
And they found the placer mine so they can just wash.
And it's already cleaned but it's just mixed.
So they wash that on the edge of the river.
A lot of people do that.
They have to work to get the money to get the gold.
But Ta-POO-low, he don't want to work.
Lazy.
And he watch the people washing the gold.
Indians, Chinamen, white people.

---

*According to Thompson speakers Louis Phillips, Suzanna Phillips, and Albert Seymour, *shil-ka-CHOOT* means "to spin oneself around and around."

He watch that
  and he can tell which one they get the most.
They wash — more money, more gold.
He know which one.
And he figure out how to get 'em and kill 'em.
When he do get 'em, throw 'em in Thompson River
  and take all the gold.

See, he get the gold that way without working for it,
  without somebody giving it to him.
He get it for nothing.
That's a good way at that time for him.
So he do that.
Nobody know.
He kill somebody and then he get the money.
Get the gold.
And whoever he kill, he throw 'em in the Thompson River.
Goodbye.
He do that four times.
He kill two white man
  and one Indian and one Chinaman.
But this Indian, the one he kill,
  he musta been coming from some different direction.
Maybe come from Bella Coola,
  or might come from Lillooet,
    some place strange because they don't miss 'em.
He know that.
You know, he know that were strange.
If he kill 'em, they will never miss around here.
They might miss 'em from where they come from,
  but not here.
But the white people,
  only the white people could missed 'em.
Not the Indians,
  because the Indians they don't care for it.
And the Chinaman, the same.
The other Chinaman, they might miss him.
But the Indians and the white people,
  they don't care for it.
So he kill the two white people,
  one Chinaman, one Indian.

269

And he get the gold
  and he got a lot of money.

And he started on the ranch
  and he got a ranch.
Have to pay for it for a lot of things, you know.
Pay cash.
Pay gold for it.
Buy the plough.
Buy the implements and things.
He don't buy the land because it's Indian reserve.
But he hired the man to do the work for 'em.
And he paid 'em money,
  so much a day and so on.
Build a fence.
Build a house.
Build a barn.
Build a cellar.
Clear the land and put in crops in the land.
He's a rancher.
And he's got two places.
He's got one place in the bottom of the Nicola River
  and another place on the summit
    between Nicola Valley to another little reserve
      before you get to Lytton up on the hillside.
Not to the top, but up halfways.
You could see that from the highway going down to the river.
You could see the buildings there.
Indians live there today.
Thompson Siding, I think that's the name.
That's above Lytton up on the hillside.
This place, it's between there — Nicola Valley and that place.
It's on top of that.
This mountain is not high, but that's the summit
  and then there's big open place, kinda swampy.
And that man, he take that place and he fence it.
That's for his place.
And he raise oats,
  raise potatoes,
    raise raspberries and rhubarb and things like that
      in that place.

And he raised wild grass.
Anyway it grow itself.
And he cut that for hay.
And he raise oats,
   raise wheat, potatoes, beets and mangolds,
      things like that.
And he got some pigs.
And he feed that to the pigs.
He's got a lot of money
   because he gets that money for nothing — that gold.
And nobody know.

And he get kinda old.
And he got sick.
He lives up in that mountain on that ranch in the summer.
But in the fall,
   he get everything what he raise
      and he put 'em in the cellar.
Keep 'em there
   and then he bring the some of 'em down in the other place.
And he got another house there.
That's the first house there at the bottom.
And that's where he spent the winter
   because there's not much snow there.
But up on the mountain,
   too much snow in the wintertime.
Springtime when the snow goes off
   and then he move up there and stay there all summer.
And he build a house up there — a barn and a fence and a corral
   and everything.

But he was living up there at the time he got sick.
And he was sick sick sick
   and he get poor poor and poor.
And he hire Indian doctor.
Indian doctor go over there and work on 'em.
No, he can't do it.
And he said to the people,
   "Maybe you hire another Indian doctor somewhere.
   My power is not good, is not enough.
   I can't get him to be good.

        Maybe other doctor might do."
So he quit.

And he get another doctor.
The same way.
And he couldn't get the right doctor.

And this man get lower and lower and lower.
And he going to die, looks like.
Somebody tell 'em
    "There was one Indian doctor at Coldwater,
        his name Chaha.
    Good doctor.
        Maybe get him.
        Bring him and he can work for 'em.
        He might make it."

So he come and take Chaha from Coldwater.
Take 'em over there.

And Chaha, he started to work for that man.
The first night he sing a song
    and he tie the handkerchief around his eyes
        to track 'em.
He followed him wherever he was,
    to bring 'em back to get better.
And he did.
But he followed him and he come in the wrong place.
Where Shteen* is.
That's where he was.
His soul is already at Shteen.
But Chaha went there and get there.
He going to bring 'em back
    but Shteen wouldn't let him take it.
So he know that was the place.
And it got hot.
Big fire.
And he cry and holler and cry.

*Shteen is the Devil.

And he cry and holler and cry.
  "My God," he says,
  "It's awful hot place where he was.
    I can't get 'em.
    And they got a big boss there.
    His boss wouldn't let me take him.
    And it's hot place.
    I can't stand it."
That's what he says when he take that handkerchief off.
But he says,
  "I not give up.
    Next night I'll go back again.
    I might get him this time."

All right.
So they wanted to make him a sweathouse that day.
He go to sweathouse.
And he build up more of his power at the sweathouse.
When he come back he got more power.
And that night goes to work for Ta-POO-low.
And he go again to Shteen.
Same way.
Shteen wouldn't let him take it.
And he was hot.
Really hot this time.
He got burned.
He come back and he said,
  "That's a bad place.
    They very hot and I got burned.
    I don't know.
    I'll make another sweathouse.
    See what I will do."
And he tell the boys,
  "Make a sweathouse for me in the afternoon.
    I'll go in the sweathouse and see what it comes."

So he go the sweathouse and never come back.
They missed him.
Getting late.
They said to some of the boys.
  "Go and see the old man, the Indian doctor."

They went over there and sweathouse is there.
Talk to him.
Never answer.
Talk to 'em.
Never answer.
They open the door.
He was laying in there,
   his head right at the door almost.
He's dead.
Died in the sweathouse.
Chaha, that's the Indian doctor.

But Ta-POO-low was alive yet at the house.

So the boys come back and they say,
   "He's dead."
And they take the stretcher.
They make a stretcher out of heavy blanket.
Put 'em on the pole.
And they went over there
   and drag 'em out from the sweathouse.
As they dragging 'em, his skin,
   it skinned right off.
Cooked.
He was cooked right in the sweathouse.
But anyway, they drag 'em out
   and put 'em on the stretcher
      and take 'em to the house
         and leave 'em there for that night.
Next day they roll 'em and pack 'em.
Pack 'em home to Coldwater.
Bury 'em.

Ta-POO-low was still alive.
He didn't die for a month or so after that.
And finally he died.
Still up there.
He figures when he get better
   then he can move down to the other place.
But he never get better.
He still there.

274

He died.
They got a lot of snow,
  about a foot and a half of snow already.
It was somewhere around maybe December.
But whoever they tell me that, they said,
  "It's not Christmas yet."
Might be in December he died.
So they going to held 'em there for three nights.
On the third day they going to bring 'em down to the bottom
  and then bury 'em.
He's dead.
They make a coffin out of the box.
When they finish the coffin,
    then they put him in the coffin
      and they cover 'em with the white rag.
Cover his head.
And he lay there.
The cabin was long.
In the other end in the corner, that's where he lay.
And the people, they cook in one end
  and they eat there.
And the rest of 'em after they eat, they be sitting there.

And that night about middle-night,
  somewhere around there,
    and all the Indians,
      (cause it's cold, there's not many, just a few),
        they all in the house.
And one of them, he says,
  "Look at that!"
And they all look.
He get up and he throw that white blanket.
Throw 'em that way and he get up.
And he sat in the box.
And he looked around.
Supposed to be the dead man.
Get up.
Come alive.

For a little while everybody just look.
Nobody say nothing.

They're all scared.
And he said,
   "All right.
   My people, anybody could come, anyone of you or more,
      whatever, they could come raise his left hand like that.
   Somebody come and shake hand with me."
And he hold 'em that way while he was sitting in the box.
And nobody went.

Again he said,
   "Anybody, any of you could come,
      one or two or more.
   Shake hand with me."

Nobody get up.
They wouldn't shake hand with him.
Three times he called.
Nobody come.

He said,
   "All right.
   Good thing for you people not to come.
   If anybody come and shake hand with me
      and that's going to be my people.
   They got to go with me.
   I'm down where Shteen is.
   I was sent back to tell this
      what I have done in my time.
   For the people to know."

But he don't say,
   "I'm going to die again."
He never did say.

So he said,
   "Now listen.
   Let me tell you what I have done.
   Nobody know.
   I know that for sure," he said.
He said,
   "I kill four person,

276

two whiteman, one Indian, one Chinaman.
I killed them and throw 'em in Thompson River.
And the gold they got, I take 'em all.
Do the same in each one.
And I had all their gold.
That's why I got money.
That's why I increase my ranch.
And that's what I have done in my life.
And that is why God says not to kill nobody.
Should not kill a person.
But I did.
I kill four.
And that is why by now I was down see Shteen.
Because that's Shteen's way.
He like it that way.
He like me that way.
That's where I was.
I come alive to tell you.
The people should know.
That's why I come alive."

He never say,
  "I'm going to die again."

So the people find that out.
And whoever they tell me about that,
  he is there.
He listen, but he's only young.
He said he's about sixteen at that time,
  or maybe fourteen only.
He wasn't sure, but he's just young man.
Just young.
Not man yet, but a big boy.
He said maybe fourteen or maybe sixteen.
And he listen.
He seen him talking.
When he finish talking
  and he get up, step over the box.
He got only underwear,
  underwear pants and underwear shirt.
No shoes.

And he walk out.
Snow is about that high outside.
Cold.
The way they say the weather was, could be zero.
It's kinda cold.
And he walk to the barn,
  couple of hundred yards to the barn from the house.
And while he was sick, before he died,
  and he says to his friend,
    "My horse, that's the best horse I got,
      was a black horse,
        keep him in the barn all the time.
      But you can ride him any day,
        but keep him in the barn and feed him hay.
      Keep him in the barn.
      Don't turn him loose."
But he don't say he need him.
But that's the way he want him,
  but he didn't know.
But anyway, this horse, it's in the barn.
He knows.
He went out and walked there.
Take the saddle and put 'em on.
And take bridle and put the bridle on 'em.
Laid 'em on and get on that horse.
And away he goes.
And the road from the barn, seems to go by that house.
Quite close to the house.
And they could heard the horse running by the house.
And down the bottom.
That's the last.
They heard 'em went that way.
That was him they think,
  but they wasn't sure because they doesn't see 'em.
In the morning they sent the boys out to look.
They said,
    "The horse is not there and the saddle not there.
    Bridle not there.
    Look at the track.
    This is where they run."
And they follow the tracks.

And the level place,
  pretty soon they went down to a steep hill.
Not too far, but he make a trail himself there.
The trail was zigzag.
And instead of that horse follow that zigzag,
  he go straight down.
He slide on the snow half of the time, but he never fall
  until he go over a lot of snow
    and he come to the bottom land.
Then he have to run about mile and a half or something like that
  to come to the other home, the other house — his.
And he stop at the door.
And the door may not locked.
Nobody know.
And he stop.
He must have stop, undo the saddle,
  and he musta push the saddle over that way.
And the saddle fall
  and they kinda upside-down.
Then he take the bridle off
  and throw 'em there.
And the horse run.
And he open the door and go in and close the door
  and lock it.
Lock the door after he get in.
And he go the other end
  and he pick up the gun that's laying there on the wall
    and he musta know they have the shells in 'em.
Or, he musta know where the shell was.
And he put shell in the bar and come back to the door
  and stand right by the door there.
And he put the gun right there.
Then he push the trigger right down there with his thumb.
Blow right through the head.
And he drop.
And he's poor.
Shake a long time.
He pretty poor.
But there's a lot of blood.
Where did that blood come from?
He lose about two gallon of blood.

279

But he's poor.
Where that blood was when he was alive?
And the blood run out by the door.
It's open a little bit, you know.
He run out just a little.
Then he froze there.
When the people come to the door,
   as soon as they come,
      it just a'coming out and they froze.
And they try the door.
It's locked.
And they have to open the window to come in.
He's lying there.
He's laying there dead.
Shot himself.
He died at the second time.
And then they open the door
   and they musta keep him somehow.
They bring the box.
They pack the box down and they put him back in the box.
Maybe the next day anyway, they bury 'em there.
That's Ta-POO-low.

See, that's the way he was.
He died but he come alive and he mention what he have done.
That's why he go to Shteen.
His soul go to Shteen because God say so.
Whenever somebody kill the other person,
   when he died, he can go to Shteen's place.
So he did.
He say so.
He mention to the people.

He says,
   "The priest tell that stories,
      and I says, 'The priest is telling lie.'
   But he's not telling lie.
   That's true.
   It was true.
   That's the way I was now to tell you so you'll
      know and tell the rest of 'em and keep telling 'em

280

so the people will know what happens with me from now on
  long time from now on."

Then right today, there's not many.
I don't think anybody know that.
But I do.
Maybe some people over there in Lytton, Spence's Bridge,
  in that area,
    they might know that.
But the people this way, they don't know anything about 'em.
But I do.

Puss in Boots

A rancher and his family have a good life until one day when a strange monster arrives on the scene.

Yeah, I'll tell you "Cat With the Boots On."
Riding boots on.
That's the stories, the first stories.
There was a big ranch, not around here.
That's someplace in European.
Overseas.
That's a long time, shortly after the "imbellable"* stories.
But this is part "imbellable" stories.
It's not Indian stories.
This is white people stories,
  because I learned this from the white people.
Not the white man.
The white man tell his son,
  that's Allison — John Fall Allison.
White man.
He is the one that tell the stories to his son.
His son, Bert Allison.
His son was a half Indian and a half white,
  because his mother was an Indian.
And his father was a white man.
So his father told him these stories.
But he told me — Bert Allison.
So he told me,
  "This is not Indian stories.
  White man stories."
You understand that?

---

*This is Harry's English translation for *chap-TEEK-whl*, stories about the world as it was during the time of the animal-people. "Imbellable" was the term adopted by Harry during a discussion with a non-native who explained to Harry that these stories were "unbelievable."

John Fall Allison, he died in 1897.
And his wife Susan died in 1937.
So he is the one that tell that story.

All right.
There's a big ranch in Europe some place.
This is a big ranch.
They got a lot of cattle and a lot of horses
   and a lot of hay land.
Everything they got.
A lot of everything.
Big ranch.
And this rancher,
   whoever they are, I didn't know his name.
That's a white man.
So he got a wife and he got two sons.
Just the four of them.
So his wife died first.
After she died
   and only the two sons and him.
The three of them.
And they still there on the house, home ranch.
Still there.
And they got a lot of man,
   a lot of hired hand to do the work.
Not close to there, but way out.
Maybe another ranch way out somewhere
   and they doing something else.
Maybe one gang, they doing nothing but branding,
   branding horses, branding cattle just for the stock, you know.
That's another gang.
And another gang just farming,
   just ploughing, seeding and irrigating.
They do that.
That's another gang.
And might be another gang,
   they doing the haying.
Do the haying in haying time.
It's quite a different gang, but they all belong to one man.
So they do that when they work.
They got a lot of men.

They were out and they eat over there.
But him and his son, they stay at home.

And one day the one guy come in and knocked on the door.
And they got a cook, him and his two sons.
And they had a hired cook,
   because the boys was just young
      and himself, he was kind of old.
And they hired a cook.
And him and his son, they don't do any work.
They just stay in the house and they don't do any work.
They got a cook.

And somebody knocked on the door.
And the cook went over there and opened the door.
And he see a man stand about six feet high.
Tall man and a big man.
And he look more like a bear.
He got hair on the body.
Not too long.
Just short hair.
And this is different, you know.
More like a gorilla.
Did you know what that is?

And, this gorilla, he told em,
   "Where's the boss?"
Mention his name.
   "Well, he's here."
   "You tell him that I want to go in
      and that I want to talk to him."

All right.
The cook come back.
And he tell the boss there was a man stood out there.
   "Big man, he want to see you.
   He want to talk to you."
He says,
   "All right, tell him to come in."

And this gorilla,

well, we call him that,
   I don't know his name,
      he come in and he go in the room.
And that's where the old man is.
And he get in there and he says,
   "Hello, I come to talk some business."
Old man says,
   "All right."
He says to the old man,
   "You got one horse out here in the yard.
   Old horse.
   And you got a cat.
   And all this ranch, it's all yours.
   You're the owner?"
He says,
   "Yeah, I'm the owner."
   "But, you got one old horse
      and you got a cat in the house here."
   "Yeah, that's right."
And he tell him,
   "Now, now is mine.
   Take that old horse and put the saddle on.
   And take your blanket.
   Take your clothes.
   Take some grub,
      just enough to pack for that old horse.
   And take the stuff you can pack from here,
      just enough for one horse.
   And take your cat and your boys.
   And you get out of here.
   You beat it.
   You move out some place
      and make a home anywhere you want to stop.
   If you don't do that
      you're going to lose your life right now.
   This is mine.
   This ranch is mine now."

Well, old man, he thought,
   Supposing if I against him.
      He going to kill me

285

and I'm going to die right now.
But if I take his word,
    I'll be alive now for sometimes.

All right, he tell his boys,
   "Let's get out of here."
So they went out and get the horse
   and bring him in close to the house.
Put the saddle on him.
And he get some grub and blanket and their clothes.
They just enough to pack that horse.
And they pack them.
And themselves, they pack some.
And away they go.
That's all.

All the rest of the ranch, it belongs to that big man.
So just like one guy did to me.
He force 'em.
He beat 'em.
Otherwise, if they don't do that, he kill him.
So he really beat 'em anyway.

So this man, old man, he moved.
They went along
   could be maybe ten miles or more.
He went away from his house
   and he see one good land.
Looks like it's very good.
He thought,
   Maybe I should make a home here.
So they stopped there,
   unload the horse
       and then they stay there.
And from there, it's not far,
   but there's a creek something like this,
       and it's on the other side of the creek.
There was another man lived there.
That's another big rancher.
That's a white man too.

So the next morning, he tell his boys,
  "We're going to make a home here.
    We're going to put up a more like a teepee."
So they can be under if it's raining.
Maybe teepee to start with.

So they make a teepee and they lived there for a while.
And in the summer,
  getting to be fall, September, or maybe August,
    and he says to his boys,
      "We should go out and cut some log."
They got some timber in the place,
  something like this.
    "We can cut some log.
     Get a log
       and then we can drag this log on that horse.
     And we get them together
       and then we can put up a log cabin.
     That's for the winter.
     We can finish the cabin.
     Winter come
       and we can be in the cabin
         so we wouldn't get cold.
     We're going to live here."

All right.
They started.
They took their axe along.
They got axe and saw and they carry them along.
So they went and cut some logs.
They cut 'em.
And they get that horse and they harness 'em.
And they took harness, and they drag this log
  to where they want to build a cabin.

And before they had enough log
  and somebody came around.
And that's from the other ranch across the creek.
That's a hired man.
He's a foreman on that ranch.
There was some other working man, but he's a foreman.

287

But he, somebody told him
   there was somebody working over here, not too far from here.
So he thought,
   Maybe I better go and see 'em
      what they're doing over there.
So he come around and he see this old man.
And he says to the old man,
   "What you been doing here?"
   "Well," the old man says,
   "I was cutting logs.
   I'm going to build a cabin."
He tell 'em all about what happened with him.
He says,
   "I gotta build a cabin
      and I'm going to live here."
So this man, he think,
   "By God, it was too bad for the old man.
   Maybe I should give him a hand.
   But I'm going to tell the head boss."

So he went back
   and get back to his boss
      and he tell his boss,
         "There was one man with two boys, just young boys,
            trying to make a home there.
         They going to build a cabin
            and they haven't got anything.
         They got only axe and cross-cut saw.
         And the boys were young.
         And the old man was kind of too old to do the work.
         But they figure they going to build a cabin.
         But I should go over there and help them."

And his boss says,
   "All right, you better take some equipment,
      tools or something.
   Take team, team of horses.
   You can drag the logs with two horses.
   Two horses team.
   And help them build the cabin.
   Do all you can for them."

All right.
The next day he come with the team of horses.
And what they cut all over the place
   and they drag them.
Get them together.
And he always work.
And everyday he come.
And they put up the cabin.
They finish the cabin.
And they make a chimney
   just like the chimney we see over there last night.
They make that chimney.

So pretty soon, winter time.
So the old man, he settle down.
He got a cabin and everything.
It could be around September then,
   when he finished the cabin.
So this man leave and he says,
   "All right.
    You all right now.
    I go back."
He come everyday, you know.
Sometimes, may not come one day, two days,
   never come.
But he come most of the time
   and help the old man.
Sometimes he bring some of the other workers
   to do some of the heavy work.

And he lived there for a couple of years.
And this ranch is across the creek.
Not very far.
And he always give him a hand for something.

So about two years they lived there.
Maybe three years.
And the old man, he was sick.
Getting old.
He was sick and sick
And pretty soon he died.

Died right there in his cabin.
And before he die, he was pretty low.
He know he was going to die.
And this man, the one that helped him all the time,
   the foreman from that other ranch,
     he always come and see him and helped him a little.
So, he says to that man,
   "I want you to be with me for the will I'm going to make."
He says, "All right."
  "So," he says,
   "I know I'm going to die not too long.
   I'm getting old and sick and I'm going to die.
   And I got nothing.
   I got only one horse,
     and a house, and a cat.
   That's all I got.
   I got two boys.
   I'll give the older boy,
     I'll give him the horse and the saddle.
   Then he got something they belong.
   He could take that,
     pack that horse and then he could go.
   But the younger boy,
     he'll be the owner of the house,
       then the cat,
         because the cat has got to stay in the house anyway.
   So, he'll be the owner for the cat and the house when I die."

So finally, maybe a few days after that,
   he die.
So after he died and was buried,
   and the older boy take the horse and saddle 'em.
Whatever he got, he packed 'em
   and lead the horse and go.
That's his, you know.
That's his horse.
He can find some place where they can live
   or whatever they can do.

But the younger boy,
   he getting bigger then, you know.

He's still in the house with the cat
   but they are poor.
He can't work.
He don't know how to work.
And I don't know how they lived,
   but they lived there anyway.

So, they were there together,
   him and his cat, for a while.
And finally the cat,
   he figure out a lot of things, you know.
He figure out.
He would like to figure out
   how he going to get the ranch back to this boy, his dad's ranch.
So he said to his master, that boy,
   he says to him,
      "I want you to go out somewhere and find me some boots.
      I want to have boots.
      That's what he's got on here.
      Riding boots I want.
      Get me a pair.
      And I can wear 'em.
      And when I wear 'em,
         I want to go out with the boots on.
      Look around.
      I want to find something."
And his master told him,
   "Those boots are worth a lot of money.
   I got no money to buy 'em."
So he tell him,
   "I want you to go and look for 'em.
   You do it.
   Look for boots.
   Bring 'em if you find 'em.
   You got to find 'em."

So anyway, this boy,
   he went out and looked around
      and asked somebody they got the boots on
         if he could have that boots.
Some of them say,

"All right, you can have them.
  This is old boots."
All right, they take 'em off.
  "You take 'em."
And they give 'em to him.
That's his thought, you know.
So, he come back with the boots.
And he tell the cat,
  "I got the boots for you."

So the cat put 'em on.
Then he went out.
Just like now today if you got a cat here,
  if it's a tomcat, stay here,
    sometimes, you don't know which way they go.
They just go out three, four days and come back.
Stay home for so long and go out again.
Two, three days and come back.
See?
It begin to be that way from that time.
So this cat went out and he come back with nothing.
But he see something out there
  and he figure out how he's going to get 'em.
So he says to his master,
  "I want you to get me,
    whatever you call that stuff,
      you can pack 'em.
  Kind of a sack, you know.
  You can put 'em over your shoulder.
  Get me a pair like that.
  I want to use 'em.
  Get me kinda stiff, not soft, you know."

  "Well," his master told him,
  "I don't think I can get 'em.
  I don't know where to get 'em."
  "Oh," he says,
  "you go out and get 'em.
  Ask somebody."

So that man went out and look around.
And finally he go to the second-hand store.
Looked around,
  and he see the one he's looking for.
And he asked the storekeeper,

292

"How much?"
"Oh, not much, fifty cents."
So he buy that bags for fifty cents.
So he take 'em home and he tell the cat,
  "I got the one you want."

The next day he put 'em on.
Put his boots on and went out.
He go to the lake,
  on the edge of the lake.
And there's wheat.
And he get some of that wheat
  and he go to the water
    and he put that bags,
      lay them on the edge of the water.
And he put some wheat inside.
Then he put the wheat along the ground by the water
  and he put them on the water.
Then he went back and he lay down
  and he watch.
And the ducks were around on the water.
Pretty soon the ducks, they were swimming around.
Swimming around till they could see the wheat.
It's on the edge of the water.
They still on the water.
Not the wheat,
  but the, what you call it?
The wheat that's in the stuff, you know, never sunk.
Still in the water.
On the water.
But the other wheat, they smash 'em.
And they pure wheat.
And he put 'em in the bag.
And the ducks, the two of 'em,
  they come and they eat that wheat.
Come out and they follow that.
And they go into that bag.
He watch 'em a little while
  and the other one go in there.
The bag is not big,
  but the both of 'em go in there.

Then he jump and sit on 'em.
And then he caught the ducks.
He kill 'em.
And when he kill 'em
  and then he put 'em in the bags
    and pack 'em and go home.
He got home in the evening
  and he said to his master,
    "I got two ducks."
So the boy,
  he think that was all right.
    "We can cook that duck and eat 'em," he said.
But the cat told him,
  "No, we not going to eat 'em.
    Tomorrow morning I'm going to go across the river,
      across the creek.
    And I'm going to give 'em these ducks
      to that rancher over there.
    I want him to eat these ducks.
    Not us.
    I'm trying to get these ducks for 'em
      because he help us
        when we build a cabin to live in.
    And we never do anything for 'em.
    But now I get that duck
      and I'm going to give it to him.
    Then I'm going to get some more things for him."

Well, the boy thinks that's not good.
  "We should eat that duck."
But the cat, he don't want.

So the next day,
  the cat, he put that in the bags
    and pack 'em and went over there.
And he come to that place.
And they had a cook.
He knocked on the door.
Just like the picture here.
He was standing like that.
Then the cook open the door

and he seen the cat standing there
    just like the way the picture was.
And he's surprised.
Kinda scared.
And the cat told 'em,
    "Don't you get that way.
    Don't you get surprised.
    I'm all right.
    I'm not going to hurt you.
    I want you to tell the boss
      I want to see him.
    I want to go in there."

All right.
The cook came back and tell the boss,
    "A cat's standing out here with the boots on.
    Looks like a man, but he's a cat.
    He want to come in to talk to you."
And this old rancher said,
    "All right.
    Let him come in."
So he come back, the cook,
    to the door and tell him,
      "All right, you go in and see him."
So he come in and go in the room.
And he say to that man,
    "I have two ducks here.
    I give you these ducks.
    You can tell your cook to fix it and cook it for you,
      make it good.
    Then you eat it.
    I am the cat.
    The owner, that man across the creek."
"All right," he says,
"Thank you.
 I eat that."

So he left.
He go home.
Next morning he went out
    and he looked around,

and he found, he seen some rabbit.
He see the rabbit running around.
Little bushy land.
Rabbit was running around.
He wonder how he going to get them.
But anyhow, he thought,
  I lay these bags here.
  Then I can hide behind them.
  They might see.
  They might think, What was that?
  They might come and look.
  They might look inside.
  I can get 'em that way.

So anyway,
  he set the bags right there.
Then he hide behind.
Not too long and the rabbit were running around.
And they see that.
Something they never seen before.
So they went over there and they get closer.
Look, and finally they go in.
The both of them look.
And they jump and he get 'em.
He kill 'em.
He go back home
  and he says to his master,
    "I get two rabbits."
So the boy think,
  He going to give 'em to that ranch across the creek.
 "Yeah, I will.
  Tomorrow I take 'em over there for him to eat that."
So the next day he went there.
And he get there and knocked on the door.
The cook notice it was the same cat.
  "All right, I got two rabbits here
    and I just come here to give 'em to the boss.
    You cook 'em and let the boss eat 'em."

So there's one more thing he done,
  but I forget.

Supposed to be three.
He get something that last,
  but I couldn't remember.

But anyway, on the third time
  he took something to that rancher,
    and then he was going to go back
      and then he tell the cook,
        "Tell him to come back.
          I want to talk to him."

So the cat was already out and the cook tell 'em,
  "He want you.
    You come back."

And he come back.
And the boss get there
  and he says to the cat,
    "Who's idea that you give me this duck
      and the rabbit
        and"
          (there's another thing,
            I couldn't remember what it was)
    "Who told you to do that?"
He says.
  "Nobody.
    I get them myself.
    And I thought I'm going to give you.
    But King,"
    (he call his master, King),
  "but King, he's at home all the time.
    King is my master but I get 'em myself."

So this man told him,
  "King.
    Maybe you can tell King
      that I'm going to drive tomorrow that way.
    I'm going to drive with a team of horses on the buggy.
    I'm going to drive that way.
    You can tell King,
      should go to the road and wait for me.

I want to take him along."
"All right," he says,
"I'll tell King."

So, he went home.
And he says to King,
    "Tomorrow morning,
        early in the morning,
            about eight o'clock in the morning,
                and that rancher is going to come on the buggy.
        And you should go to that road,
            close to the creek.
        He want to take you along.
        He's going out for a drive.
        He want to take you along," he says.

Well King, he says,
    "Well, what do I have to go over there for?"
    "He says you got to go. He want you to go."
    "All right," he says, "All right, I'll go."

So in the morning he says to King,
    "I think you should take a bath
        before you catch a ride with that rancher."
And King, he says,
    "It's too cold to take a bath."
He says to King,
    "You're going to take a bath at the creek,
        right in the cold water.
    And then the road, it come across the creek.
    And while you take a bath,
        when you get through and you just wait there.
    When he come, you go along with him.
    You go along with him and I go along.
    I run.
    We can both go."

All right.
He says, King, he says,
    "It's cold."
    "Ah," he says, "you better go take a bath."

So they went.
And this is a crossing, a road across the creek.
And water was running and kind of turning there.
Deep water.
Turns like,
  and then it goes like.
King, he takes his clothes off.
And he says to King,
  "You jump in the water
    and you swim across and then back."

It's quite big.
The water was kind of circle there.
And King is supposed to swim across and then back.
King, he get on the water and swim.
And while he swim that way
  and then the cat take his clothes
    and throw 'em in the creek.
Then King come out.
His clothes is not there!

He says,
  "Where's my clothes?"
And the cat told him,
  "The wind was blowing
    and it blow them
      and they get on the water and down they went.
    You could just see 'em.
    They quite a ways already.
    You lose 'em.
    You can never get 'em."
He's naked!
No clothes!

Well, he was cold.
Then King told 'em,
  "You better go back to the house
    and get matches and we can make fire.
    Get me clothes from there."

So while he was saying that,

he see the buggy coming.
He says to King,
   "This is your partner.
    He's coming already."
   "Well," King says, "I got no clothes.
    I can't go along."
Anyway, when the buggy stopped there and they asked,
   "What's the matter? Who's that?"
Cat says,
   "That's King."
   "What's happened? Why does he have no clothes?"
   "Well," he says, "he's taking a bath
    because he's going along with you.
    And he take a bath, take his clothes off
     and he put 'em here.
    And while he swim over there,
     the wind blow.
    And then blow the clothes.
    And down they went on the creek."
And the rancher tell 'em,
   "My God, that's too bad.
    He lost his clothes."
So he says,
   "Just wait here.
    We go right back.
    I got some extra clothes.
    I can bring some clothes for him."
So they wait there.
King, he's got no clothes.
So they went back,
  just the two of them.
Him and his driver.
And he get to his house.
And he tell his wife,
   "Get me some clothes.
    Suit of clothes and underwear and shirt and pants and coat,
     suit of clothes and hat, shoes.
    King, he's got no clothes
     and I'm going to give him these clothes."
So his wife get all his clothes.

So the king, he get the clothes.
I mean the rancher, he take him the clothes
   and give 'em to King.

And he's got two daughters.
Good looking girls.
Young girls.
And he says to his wife,
   "I think I should take the girls along with us
      so they could see a lot of things.
      Come back in the evening."
   "Well," she says, "all right."
She tell her daughters,
   "You better go with Dad."

Well the girls, they glad to go along
   because they get to see the country.
So he take the two girls.
And they got two seat in the buggy.
You know, the front seat,
   that's where the rancher and his driver.
And the girls in the back seat.
Just like the car, you know.
So they went out.
When they come to King,
   well, King stood there no clothes.
And he give 'em that clothes.
Tell 'em,
   "You put this on.
   When you get these clothes on,
      you get on the buggy and you go along with me.
   I want you to come."

So King,
   he put the underwear on and pants and coat and nice hat.
And so he says to King,
   "You could sit there in between these two girls.
   Then you keep the both of them warm.
   And you could sit in between them.
   And you get warm from you each side."
King was shaking cold.

All right.
King get on the buggy.
And then the girls go apart
  and King was sitting in between.
Then he put some blanket so he'll get warm.
Then they go.

And the cat, they don't know.
Awhile he was there
  and then he's gone.
Nobody know which way it went.
But anyway, the cat was ahead of them,
  a long ways ahead of them.
And he come to the place where they got a lot of cattle.
They have 'em in corral
They branding them.
Branding calves.
He come to that place.
Bunch of men working.
They he stop and he looked at 'em.
All the men, they were surprised to see a cat look like that.
And he says to one of 'em,
  "Do you guys had a boss here?"
  "Yeah, we got a boss."
  "Tell him to come. I want to see him."
Well, that's the foreman in that outfit.
So they tell him and he come.
The cat says to him,
  "You're the boss?"
  "Yeah, well I'm a foreman running this."
He says to that boss,
  "Kings, they two kings,
    one king on the front seat with his driver,
    and the other king on the hindseat with two girls.
  They going to get here in a little while.
  When they get here, they're going to stop
    and they're going to ask you, they're going to tell you,
      'Who own this cattle?
      Who's the owner?
      You're working for who?'
  If they ask you, you can tell them,

I'm working for somebody.
And they could tell you,
  'Who's the owner?
   You're working for who?'
Then you could tell them,
  'I'm working for King.'
You can mention,
  'That king, the one that's in the hindseat.'"

That's what the cat told 'em.
Told 'em,
  "You can tell them you're working for King.
  You mention that king.
  It's in the hindseat.
  That's the king you're working for.
  That's what you have to tell the other king on the front.
  If you don't do that,
    something is going to happen with you.
  You have to say that."
That's what the cat says to that boss.
And the boss said,
  "All right, I'll do that."

So he went.
Run ahead of 'em before the buggy came.
And he went to the next bunch.
There was a next bunch working there.
So after awhile,
  and they see the buggy coming.
And it come
  and then it stop there.
Then that boss, the foreman is not far.
Then he ask, the king, he ask,
  Well the rancher, you know.
But the cat, he call 'em kings.
Two kings.
And he says,
  "Who is there?
   Got any boss here?"
  "Yeah."
  "Where is the boss?

I want to see him."
He tell 'em and then he come.
  "You're the boss?"
  "I'm the foreman.
   I'm running this outfit."
  "Who are you working for?"
  "I working for King there.
   I working for him.
   He's the owner."
By God, he put it down on the paper.

All right.
They went away.

And the cat,
  he keep running and running and running.
Come to the bunch of mans working at the hay, you know.
Hay gang.
So they stop there.
And all the boys looking at the cat.
Look like this, this picture.
[Harry points to the picture of "Puss in Boots" on the catfood tin.]
Surprised to see the cat like that.
He's big, you know.
Not small.
About this high.
He had that clothes on.
Boots.
They surprise to see that.
Anyway, he ask,
  "Do you guys have any boss here?"
  "Yeah, there's one here."
  "Tell him to come.
   I want to talk to him."
He tell 'em the same thing.
He says
  "There's a buggy coming
    with two kings in there.
   One king in the front with the driver,
     and the other king in the hindseat with two girls.
   When they get here, they can ask you.

304

Then you can tell 'em you're working for the king,
    the one that's in behind.
If you don't do that,
    something is going to happen with you.
You better take my word."
So they said,
  "All right, I'll do that."

So they went.

And after awhile and the buggy come,
  and they stopped there
  and they asked for the foreman, the boss.
"Tell him to come."
And they asked him,
  "You running a job here?"
  "Yeah."
  "You're working for who?
  Who? Who's the owner?"
  "King.
  He is the owner.
  I working for King."
Well, that's his dad's outfit in the first place
  and that cat,
    he want to get that back to King,
      the second king.
So they do the same thing again
  in a lot of places.
They come to a place where they branding horses.
They say the same thing.
Then they come to the place
  where they ploughing and disking.
And bunch of them,
  they come to a place where they thrash the grain,
    maybe wheat, oats, something like that.
Running the thrashing machine.
Bunch of them.
They tell the same thing.
And they all do the same.
They all say,
  "I work for King."

305

So this other king,
   the one that's on the front,
     by God, he think King is well off.
It's too bad he pretty near die this morning, by cold.
So at last they come to the house,
   to the home ranch.
That's his dad.
King's dad.
That's the house they go away from there.
It was still there.
So they come to that place.

And they got a cook.
Then the cat, he come to the door.
Knocked at the door.
And then the cook went out and he see the cat.
And he scared.
Kinda jumped like he's going to run away.
Told 'em not to get surprised.
   "I want to talk to you."
Stop, and he says,
   "Where's the boss?"
   "In the house, in the room," he says.
The cat says to the cook,
   "You go over there and tell him I want to come in.
   I want to go in there in his room.
   I want to talk to him."
The cook, he went in there and he says to that man,
   "A cat was standing there.
   He want to come in here.
   He want to talk to you,
     well, not in the bedroom, but in the sitting room."
   "All right, tell him to come."
So, the cat went in there.
And this man was tall.
Big man.
And he's a monster.
He don't care.
He can kill anybody.
He's a big man.
Gorilla.

So this big man told the cat,
　"What did you come in here for?
　What did you want?"
Well, the cat, he said,
　"I got a question.
　I want to question you."
He says,
　"All right, you can question me anytime."
So the cat says,
　"I understand the people talked about you,
　　and I understand you are a big man."
　"Yeah, I am a big man."
　"And I understand that you can change yourself
　　into a something.
　Could you do that?" he says to that man.
And, this gorilla, he said,
　"Yeah, I can do that.
　I can change my body to any animal you want me to be.
　I can be that way."

All right.
Cat, he says,
　"I like to see you get changed into a lion.
　And I like to see."
　"All right," he says, "don't you get scared, though.
　You just stay still there and I'll change.
　But don't get scared.
　I'm not going to hurt you.
　But you might get scared.
　But don't scared."

So the cat stood there still.
And this other guy just make a turn and circle around.
Turn around.
Then he was a big lion.
Stand about this high.
He walked over there
　and he came back.
And he walked towards him, towards the cat.
And the cat is scared.
And he says,

307

"You better not get near me.
  Try to change back into what you are, into a person."
All right.
This one he change and he's a gorilla again.
So he stood awhile talking to 'em.
And he said,
  "I see that.
    I prove that because I seen it.
You changed into a lion
  and you're pretty big."
He says,
  "Can you change to be small?"
  "Oh yeah, I can change to a small animal."
  "All right," he say,
  "I like to see you change to be a squirrel."
That squirrel is small.
That is what your dog is after all day today.
[Harry refers to my dog, Rufus]
  "I like to see you do that."
  "All right."
So they stood there
  and this gorilla turn around twice.
And he was a little squirrel.
And he run after the wall and come back.
And the cat says,
  "All right, that's enough.
  I know that.
  I can see.
  I prove that you can do it.
  There's one more thing.
  You change into a lion.
  You're big.
  And you changed into a squirrel
    and you pretty small.
  But can you change to be a mouse?
  That's still smaller animal."
  "All right, I can change to be a mouse.
  I can change to be very little if you want."
  "Well," he says,
  "I like to see you change yourself into a mouse."
All right.

He make a turn twice
  and there was a little mouse, just small.
Then he told him,
  "First, when you get to be a mouse,
    you can run and go under."
Something like that.
They can go under there.
  "Then you can stay under there.
    And after awhile you can come out
      and run across the floor.
    And you can go under in the other part.
    I like to watch that."

So this one here turn into a mouse
  and then he run over there, under.
After awhile he peek out.
That's why the mouse do that.
You can see them now.
They get under.
Pretty soon they peek out again.
Then he come out and he run to another one.
Get under.
And he peek out.
And he says,
  "Run back again to that other place."
And he run.
And he run after him.
Before he get under
  and he got him.
And he bite him.
And he swallow him right there.
He bite on the head.
And he just chew the head and swallowed him.
No more gorilla!
He had 'em inside.
Just him there.

Then the king, he never come yet.

Then he says to the cook,
  "You better come in."

And the cook come in.
Looked around.
The boss is not there.
And he says to the cook,
   "Look at that floor there.
   See a little blood?
   Little blood on that floor?"
And the cook looked over there
   and there was a little blood.
That's where he grab him.
Smashed the head and then swallow him.
He says,
   "That's where I kill your boss.
   He change himself to a mouse and I kill him.
   I throw his head and that's the blood.
   And I swallow him.
   He's in here now.
   No more boss.
   Pretty soon the buggy is coming.
   There are two kings on that buggy,
      one on the front with the driver,
         and one on the hindseat with two girls.
   When they get here,
      they'll come here pretty soon,
         when they get here, this king,
            the one that's on the front with the driver,
               he could ask you and you could tell 'em,
                  can ask you,
                     'Who you're working?
                      Who's house this is?
                      Who's the owner?'
   You can tell them,
      'King.'
   You mention that king, the one that's in the hindseat.
   If you don't do that,
      something is going to happen to you right now.
   But you got to do what I say.
   And I'll stay right in the house."
That's what he says.

So the cook is kind of scared

because he knows his boss is dead.
Cat swallowed him.
Kill him.
And there's blood there.
He got to say what he was told by the cat.

So after awhile, he see the buggy.
And it stop on the front of the door.
And he went out there.
And the king, the one that's on the front, asked him,
   "Who's place is this?"
   "It's King's."
   "It's King's house?"
   "Yeah."
   "Which king?"
   "The one that's behind the seat there.
    That's his house.
    He is the owner."

So the one,
   the king on the front,
      he write that down.
         "King is well off.
            He's got a lot of cattle, big ranch.
            Good house."
He was visiting the place of king,
   the one that pretty near drown in the morning.
So the cook says to them,
   "Get off."
And he tell the driver to put the horses in the barn
   and feed 'em.
      "And all you come into the house."
So the driver went over there and unhooked the horses.
Feed 'em.
And he come back
   and they all go into the house.
And the cat, he says,
   he says to that king, the one that's on the front,
      "Now you know that king there,
         the one that's with you,
            he is the owner.

All what you have seen when you come around,
   the working men, that's his hired men.
All his outfit.
And this is his house.
I want to tell you that," he says.

So, the other king, he says,
  "Well, that was all right.
   Good thing I save his life.
   If I don't give him clothes right away,
      they'll be, he'll die by cold, King."
So finally he figure out.
And he says to the king, that rancher,
  he says to the king,
     "I find out now this is your house.
      And all this is all yours.
      You got a big ranch,
         but you got no wife.
      And I got two girls there.
      You can pick one of 'em.
      If you want the older one,
         you take her for your wife.
      If you want the younger one,
         you take her for your wife.
      And then we'll go, and your wife will be here."

So King, he make up his mind.
And he think,
  "I better take the older one.
   She wise.
   She smart.
   She can do the cooking.
   She can do the work.
   But the younger one is not much good.
   Too young."
So he says to the other king,
  "I'll take the older one."
All right.
He tell his daughter,
  "Now you stay here with King.
   That was your husband now."

All right.
So they go back.
But King and that cat,
  and the King got a wife,
    and the cat says to the king,
      "Now I get the ranch back to you.
     It is your dad's place.
     That's his ranch.
     You remember when that man chase you out of here?
     Take everything.
     Now I kill him.
     Turn into a mouse.
     Change into a mouse and I kill him.
     I figure that out for a long time.
     That's the reason I ask you to get me the boots,
       to get me that bag.
     I figure that way.
     And I treat him good, that king,
       so he can come.
     That's my figure.
     Now you get the ranch back.
     It's yours."
He says,
  "All what I have to get,
   I can stay in the house here.
   I can lay down in the bed anywhere I want.
  Don't kick me out of the bed.
  And don't kick me out of good stuff if I lay there.
  You can feed me good.
  Give me something to eat.
  Anything, meat, fish,
   give me that for me to eat.
  Then I can stay in the house.
  If I want to go out, I go out.
  Pretty soon I come in
   and I can lay down anyplace.
  And you pat me.
  And you be good to me at all time.
  But if you're not good to me,
   if you kick me,
    if you take the broom and chase me out with the broom

313

or something,
        you going to have another bad luck.
    And it's going to be bad for you
        for the rest of your time.
    But if you treat me right,
        you can be all right at all time."

So that is the reason why now at anyplace,
    you come to the house where some people they got a cat,
        then you can see the cat,
            they lay there,
                or they could lay on the bed,
                    or they could lay right on the pillow.
They can lay at anyplace.
Whoever owned the cat, they let them stay there.
They can do as they like.
That's the reason why.
Because in another way, he is the owner.
If you treat them bad, you get bad luck.
Once they give you bad luck,
    they going to give you bad luck the rest of your time.
But if you've got a cat, you should treat him right.
If it's young, it can make a damage here
    and don't be mad at him that way.
That is why your cat,
    you got to treat him right.
Because he figures, he is the owner.
Whatever you have.
Not only you, but anybody.
Anybody had a big ranch,
    or anybody had a lot of money, well off, you know,
        that's supposed to be belong to the cat.
If you don't treat your cat right,
    you're going to lose that.
You wouldn't know how,
    but you're going to get in a bad way.
You're going to get in bad luck.
First thing you know, you'll have nothing.
Got to treat the cat right.

That's the way it's supposed to be.

A lot of people, they don't know that.
Some people, they don't like cats.
Supposing if the cat's here, they'd kick 'em out.
So that's not good.
But some people they don't know anyway,
  because they don't know.
But as long as you know that,
  you should be good to your cat.
In another way, you shouldn't have cat,
  so you wouldn't have to fight with nothing, you know.

You treat your dog very good.
You can do the same with your cat.
There are stories for the dog, too.

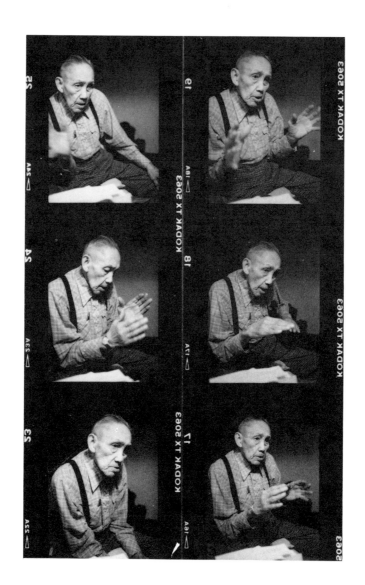

Harry telling stories, October, 1985.

ACKNOWLEDGEMENTS

I would like to thank the Explorations Programme of the Canada Council for providing the funding necessary for the preparation of this manuscript. Richard Holden of the Explorations Programme was particularly interested in the stories, and I appreciate his support throughout our work on it. I also extend my gratitude to the Phillips Fund, of the American Philosophical Society, Philadelphia, and to the Canadian Ethnology Service of the Canadian Museum of Civilization, Ottawa, for their funding of field research in 1981 and 1982 during which some of these stories were recorded. Special thanks go to Robert Semeniuk who made a trip to the Similkameen Valley in October, 1985 to photograph Harry. Patricia Walker used these photographs in her work on the design of the cover, and this work is much appreciated. Special thanks also go to Karl Siegler, Jeff Derksen, and Michael Barnholden of Talonbooks and Jeff Smith of Theytus Books for undertaking this project and seeing it through to completion.

I would personally like to thank Randy Bouchard and Dorothy Kennedy of the British Columbia Indian Language Project for first introducing me to Harry in 1977. Carole Carpenter, Blanca Chester, Dr. A.C.R. M'Gonigle and Karl Siegler provided thoughtful editorial suggestions. I would also like to thank Michael M'Gonigle, my husband, who has shared with me many hours of listening to Harry's stories.

Finally, I would like to thank Harry Robinson. This book represents many hours of his time and a gracious sharing of his knowledge.

Wendy Wickwire
Vancouver, B.C.